CHILDHOOD

BY THE SAME AUTHOR

NOVELS

Portrait of a Man Unknown
Martereau
The Planetarium
The Golden Fruits
Between Life and Death
Do You Hear Them?
"Fools Say"

SHORT PROSE AND CRITICISM

Tropisms
The Age of Suspicion
The Use of Speech

PLAYS

Collected Plays: *Silence, The Lie, It is
There, Izzum* and *It's
Beautiful*

CHILDHOOD

Nathalie Sarraute

Translated by Barbara Wright
in consultation with the author

GEORGE BRAZILLER / New York

Published in the United States in 1984 by George Braziller, Inc.

Originally published in France in 1983 as *Enfance*
by Editions Gallimard, 5 rue Sebastien-Bottin, 75341 Paris.

For information address the publisher:
    George Braziller, Inc.
    One Park Avenue
    New York, NY 10016

Designed by Levavi & Levavi

Library of Congress Cataloging in Publication Data

Sarraute, Nathalie.
    Childhood : an autobiography.

    Translation of: Enfance.
    1. Sarraute, Nathalie—Biography—Youth.   2. Novelists,
French—20th century—Biography.   I. Title.
PQ2637.A783Z46413   1984   848'.91409   [B]   83-20864
ISBN 0-8076-1085-2

Text design: Rucith Ottiger/Levavi & Levavi

Printed in the United States of America

CHILDHOOD

Then you really are going to do that? "Evoke your childhood memories"... How these words embarrass you, you don't like them. But you have to admit that they are the only appropriate words. You want to "evoke your memories"... there's no getting away from it, that's what it is.

—Yes, I can't help it, it tempts me, I don't know why...

—It could be... mightn't it be... we sometimes don't realize... it could be that your forces are declining...

—No, I don't think so... at least I don't feel they are...

—And yet what you want to do... "to evoke your memories"... mightn't that be...

—Oh, for heaven's sake...

—Yes, the question has to be asked: wouldn't that mean

that you were retiring? standing aside? abandoning your element, in which up to now, as best you could...

—Yes, as you say, as best I could...

—Perhaps, but it's the only one you have ever been able to live in... the one...

—Oh, what's the use? I know all about that.

—Is that true? Have you really not forgotten what it was like there? how everything there fluctuates, alters, escapes... you grope your way along, forever searching, straining... towards what? what is it? it's like nothing else... no one talks about it... it evades you, you grasp it as best you can, you push it... where? no matter where, so long as it eventually finds some fertile ground where it can develop, where it can perhaps manage to live... My goodness, just thinking about it...

—Yes, it makes you grandiloquent. I would even say, presumptuous. I wonder whether it isn't still that same fear... Remember the way it returns whenever anything inchoate crops up... What remains with us of former endeavors always seems to have the advantage over what is still trembling somewhere in limbo...

—That's just it: what I'm afraid of, this time, is that it isn't trembling... not enough... that it has become fixed once and for all, "a sure thing," decided in advance...

—Don't worry about it having been decided in advance... it's still vacillating, no written word, no word of any sort has yet touched it, I think it *is* still faintly quivering... outside words... as usual... little bits of something still alive... I would like... before they disappear... let me...

—Right. I won't say any more... and in any case, we know very well that when something starts haunting you...

—Yes, and this time, it's hardly believable, but it was you who prompted me, for some time now you have been inciting me...

—I?

—Yes, you, by your admonitions, your warnings... you conjure it up, you immerse me in it...

Nein, das tust du nicht... "No, you're not to do that"... here they are again, these words, they have come to life again, just as living, just as potent as they were at that moment, such a long time ago, when they penetrated me, they press, they bear down with all their strength, with all their enormous weight... and under their pressure, something within me that is just as strong, that is even stronger, emerges, swells, rises up... the words that come out of my mouth carry it, hammer it in... *Doch, ich werde es tun.* "Yes, I *am* going to do it."

Nein, das tust du nicht. "No, you're not to do that"... these words come from a figure that time has almost effaced... all that remains is a presence... that of a young woman sitting back in an armchair in the lounge of an hotel, where my father was spending his holidays alone with me in Switzerland, in Interlaken or Beatenberg, I must have been five or six, and the young woman had been engaged to look after me and to teach me German... I can't make her out very well, but I can distinctly see her work basket on her knees, and on top of it, a pair of steel scissors... and me... I can't see myself, but I can feel it as if I were doing it now... I suddenly seize the scissors, I grip them in my hand... heavy, closed scissors... I aim them, the point upwards, at the back of a settee covered in a delightful silk material with a leafy pattern, in a slightly faded blue, with satiny glints... and I say in German... *Ich werde es zerreissen.*

—In German... How could you have learnt it so well?

—Yes, I wonder... But those words, which I have never said since... *Ich werde es zerreissen...* "I'm going to slash it"... the word *zerreissen* has a hissing, ferocious sound, in one second something is going to happen... I'm going to slash, devastate, destroy... it will be an outrage... a criminal attack... but it won't be punished as it might be, I know there will be no penalty... perhaps just a slight reprimand, my father will look displeased, a little worried... What have you done, Tashok, what came over you? and the young woman will be indignant... but a kind of fear, stronger than that of improbable, unthinkable punishments, is still holding me back from what is going to happen in an instant... the irreversible, the impossible... what is never done, what cannot be done, no one would dare...

Ich werde es zerreissen. "I'm going to slash it"... I'm warning you, I'm going to take the plunge, leap out of this decent, inhabited, warm, gentle world, I'm going to wrench myself out of it, fall, sink into the uninhabited, into the void...

"I'm going to slash it"... I have to warn you, to give you time to stop me, to hold me back... "I'm going to slash it"... I shall say that to her very loudly... perhaps she will shrug her shoulders, lower her head, look thoughtfully at her work... Who takes it seriously when children indulge in these provocative, teasing acts?... and my words will waver, dissolve, my limp arm will drop, I shall put the scissors back in their place, in the basket...

But she raises her head, she looks me in the eyes and says, strongly stressing each syllable: *Nein, das tust du nicht...* "No, you're not to do that"... exercising a gentle, firm, insistent, inexorable pressure, the same pressure I later perceived in the words, the tone, of hypnotists, of animal tamers...

"No, you're not to do that"... these words flow in a

heavy, massive tide, what it carries with it sinks into me in order to crush what is stirring in me, what is trying to rise... and under this pressure, it braces itself, rises more vigorously, rises higher, grows, and violently projects out of me the words... "Yes, I'm going to do it."

"No, you're not to do that"... these words surround me, constrain me, shackle me, I struggle... "Yes, I'm going to do it"... There now, I'm freeing myself, excitement and exaltation impel my arm, I plunge the point of the scissors in with all my strength, the silk gives, tears, I slash the back of the settee from top to bottom, and I look at what comes out of it... something flabby, greyish, is escaping from the slit...

In that hotel... or in another Swiss hotel of the same type, where my father is once again spending his holidays with me, I am sitting at a table in a room lit by wide bay windows through which you can see lawns, trees... It's the children's dining room, where they have their meals under the supervision of their governesses, their maids.

They are sitting in a group as far away from me as possible, at the other end of the long table... the faces of some of them are grotesquely deformed by an enormous, swollen cheek... I hear guffaws, I see the amused glances they secretly dart at me, I can't quite hear, but I can guess what the adults are whispering to them: "Come on, eat up, stop that idiotic game, don't look at that child, you mustn't imitate her, she's an insufferable child, a crazy child, a fanatical child..."

—You already knew those words...

—My goodness, yes... I'd heard them often enough... But none of those vaguely terrifying, degrading words, no attempt at persuasion, no entreaty could incite me to open my mouth to accept the bit of food being impatiently waved around on the end of a fork, there, just outside my clenched lips... When I finally unclench them to admit this morsel, I immediately push it into my already full, swollen, taut cheek... a larder in which it will have to wait its turn to pass through my teeth and be masticated there until it has become *as liquid as soup*...

As liquid as soup were the words pronounced by a Paris doctor, Doctor Kervilly...

—It's curious that his name comes back to you at once, whereas so many others, however hard you try to recall them...

—Yes, I don't know why out of so many forgotten names his should surface... My mother had had me examined by him, for I don't know what minor ailments, just before I left to join my father... Which makes me think, since at that moment she lived in Paris with me, that I must have been under six...

"You heard what Doctor Kervilly said? You must chew your food until it has become *as liquid as soup*... Whatever you do, don't forget that when you're there, without me, no one there will know, they'll forget, they won't bother, it will be up to you to bear it in mind, you must remember what I'm telling you... promise me you'll do that..." "Yes, I promise, Mama, don't worry, set your mind at rest, you can rely on me..." Yes, she can be quite sure of that, I shall replace her at my side, she won't leave me, it will be as if she were still there to preserve me from the dangers that the others here are not aware of, how could they be aware of them? she is the only one who can know what's right for me, she's the only one who can distinguish what's good for me from what is bad.

It's no use telling them, explaining to them... *"As liquid as soup...* it was the doctor, it was Mama who told me that, I promised her..." They shake their heads, they smile condescendingly, they don't believe it... "Yes, yes, all right, but even so, be quick, eat up..." But I can't, I am the only one here who knows, I am the only judge here... who else here can decide for me, allow me... when the moment still hasn't come... I'm chewing as fast as I can, I assure you, my cheeks are hurting, I don't like to keep you waiting but I can't help it: it still hasn't become *as liquid as soup...* They get impatient, they try to hurry me... what do they care what she said? she doesn't count here... I'm the only one here who takes her into account...

Now, when I have my meals, the children's dining room is empty, I have them either before or after the others... I was setting them a bad example, there have been complaints from the parents... but I don't care... I'm still here, at my post... I'm resisting... I'm holding out on this bit of territory on which I have hoisted her colours, on which I've put up her flag...

—Images, words, which obviously couldn't have come into your head at that age...

—Of course not. No more than they could have come into the head of an adult... It was, as always, an all-embracing feeling, outside words... But it is these words and images that enable us to grasp, as best we can, to retain these sensations.

If I give in, if I swallow this mouthful without first having made it *as liquid as soup*, I shall be perpetrating something which I shall never be able to confess to her when I'm back there with her... I shall have to carry it hidden within me, this cowardice, this treachery.

If she was with me, I should have been able to forget about it long ago, and swallow without chewing, as I used to. My mother herself, as I knew her, insouciant and absent-minded, would soon have forgotten... but she isn't here, she made me bring that with me... *as liquid as soup*... I received it from her, she gave it to me to keep, I must conserve it piously, preserve it from all touch... Is it really what may be called *as liquid as soup* yet? isn't it still too thick? No, I really think I can allow myself to swallow it... and then bring the next piece out of my cheek...

I am very sorry to be such a nuisance to a person who is so gentle and patient, to run the risk of upsetting my father... but I have come from a long way away, from a foreign place to which they have no access, whose laws they are ignorant of, laws which, when I am there, I can amuse myself by flouting, I do sometimes infringe them, but here, loyalty obliges me to submit to them... I valiantly endure the reprimands, the mockery, the exclusion, the accusations of naughtiness, the anxiety my folly produces here, the sense of guilt... but what is that in comparison with the guilt I would feel if, going back on my promise, mocking the words which have become sacred, losing all sense of duty, of responsibility, behaving like a feeble little child, I agreed to swallow that mouthful before it had become *as liquid as soup*.

And all this was obliterated the moment I was back in Paris with my mother... once again everything took on that air of insouciance...

—It emanated from her.

—Yes, she was always a little childish, frivolous... she came to life, she shone, when she was talking to her husband or discussing things with their friends in the evenings, in the rather dark, barely furnished little flat in the rue Flatters, but she didn't seem to notice that and I didn't pay much attention to it, I liked to stay with them, just listening to them without understanding, until the moment when their voices became strange, as if more and more distant, and I vaguely felt myself being picked up, carried away...

Just to the left of the steps going up to the broad path leading to the place Médicis, under the statue of a Queen of France, beside the enormous, green-painted tub in which an orange tree is growing... with in front of me the circular ornamental lake on which boats are sailing, round which carts upholstered in red velvet and pulled by goats are circulating... with my back close up against the warmth of her leg under the long skirt... I can no longer hear the sound of her voice as it was in those days, but what does come back to me is the impression that, rather than to me, it's to someone else that she is telling... no doubt one of the children's stories she writes at home on big pages covered in her large handwriting with its disconnected letters... or is she composing it in her head... the words addressed elsewhere flow... I can, if I wish, grasp them in passing, I can let them pass by, nothing is demanded of me, no look is trying to see whether I am really listening, whether I understand... I can let myself go, I can allow myself to be immersed in that golden light, that cooing, that chirruping, the tinkling of the little bells on the heads of the donkeys and the goats, the jingling of the hoops fitted with handles that the children bowl in front of them, the very small children who don't know how to use a stick...

—Don't be angry, but don't you think that there, with that cooing, that chirruping, you haven't been able to resist introducing something a little bit prefabricated... it's so tempting, you've inserted a pretty little piece... completely in keeping...

—Yes, I may perhaps have let myself go a little...

—Naturally, how can one resist so much charm... those

12

pretty sonorities... cooing... chirruping...

—Yes, you're right... but so far as the little bells are concerned, no, not there, I can hear them... and also the
rattling sounds, the rasping sound of the red, pink, mauve
celluloid sails of the toy windmills, revolving in the wind...

I can run, gambol, go round in circles, I have plenty of time... The wall of the boulevard de Port-Royal that we are walking along is very long... it's only when we get to a side street that I have to stop and hold her hand to cross it... I get there before the maid, to give myself time to fill my lungs, so that I won't have to breathe in that atrocious smell... it immediately makes me feel sick... that emanates from her hair, which is saturated in vinegar. This enables me to hold her hand, as if there was nothing to it, without running the risk of vexing her... it isn't even so sure that she would be vexed, she's very nice and very simple, she knows that it isn't my fault if I can't stand the smell of vinegar, but neither is it her fault if outings in the fresh air give her headaches from which vinegar alone can protect her... So we had agreed that I could stay quite far away from her, except, of course, when crossing the road...

Here she is, coming nearer, a shapeless mass, her head covered with a greyish headscarf, she reaches me, she holds out her hand and I put my hand in hers... my lungs are full of air, I don't need to breathe in... I don't breathe until the moment we set foot on the pavement on the other side of the road... once there, I immediately let go of her hand and dart off... If by ill luck it happens that I haven't taken in enough air to hold out for the whole of the crossing, it's out of the question for me to hold my nose... even though she has given me permission... but it is impossible for me to do so... I can just take in tiny breaths with my head averted, but without averting it too far, that might make her guess the repulsion I feel... not towards her, not towards what she is, not at all towards what there is in her, but only towards what sometimes appears under her loosely tied scarf, the shiny, yellowish skin of her skull between the strands of her saturated hair.

Once through the gates of the Grand Luxembourg gardens, with no more roads to be ingeniously crossed, she sits down not far from the lake, her back to the vast white façade... I can't tell the time on the big clock so I don't know whether it is teatime, but I observe the other children, and the moment I see one being given his bun and bar of chocolate I rush up... she has seen me coming, she hands me mine, I grab them, thank her with a nod and go off...

—To do what?

—Ah, don't try to set a trap for me... To do anything, what children do when they play, run around, push their boats, their hoops, skip, stop abruptly and gaze intently at the other children, at the people sitting on the stone benches or the chairs... they plant themselves down in front of them, open-mouthed...

—Perhaps you did that more than the others, perhaps in a different way...

—No, I wouldn't say that... I did it in the same way as a lot of children do... and probably with observations and reflections of the same order... in any case, nothing of that has remained with me, and *you* certainly aren't going to push me into trying to plaster over that gap.

Outside that luminous, dazzling, vibrant garden, everything seems to be covered in a pall of greyness, it has a rather dismal, or rather, a sort of cramped air... but it is never sad. Not even what I still remember of the nursery school... a bare courtyard surrounded by high, sombre walls, round which we marched in Indian file, dressed in black overalls and wearing clogs.

Here, however, looming up out of that mist, is the sudden violence of terror, of horror... I scream, I struggle... what has happened? what is happening to me?

"Your grandmother is coming to see you"... Mama told me that... My grandmother? Papa's mother? Is that possible? is she really going to come? she never comes, she is so far away... I don't remember her at all, but I feel her presence in the affectionate little letters she sends me from over there, in the softwood boxes with pretty pictures carved in them, whose hollowed-out contours you can trace with your finger, in the painted wooden cups covered by a varnish that is soft to the touch... "When will she come? when will she be here?"... "Tomorrow afternoon... You won't go out for your walk..."

I wait, I watch out for her, I listen to the footsteps on the stairs, on the landing... there, here she is, the bell has rung, I want to rush out, I'm stopped, wait, don't move... the door to my room opens, a man and a woman dressed in white overalls grab hold of me, I've been put on someone's knees, I'm being held, I struggle, they press a piece of cotton wool over my mouth, over my nose, a mask, from which something atrocious, asphyxiating, emanates, suffocates me, fills my lungs, rises to my head, dying, that's what it is, I'm dying... And then, I am alive again, I'm in my bed, my throat is burning, my tears are flowing, Mama is wiping them away... "My little kitten, you had to have an operation, you know, they took something out of your throat, it was harming you, it was bad for you... go to sleep now, it's all over..."

How long did it take you to realize that she never tried—unless very absent-mindedly and clumsily—to put herself in your place?...

—Yes, curiously enough that indifference, that casualness, were part of her charm, in the literal sense of the word, she charmed me... No word, however powerfully uttered, has ever sunk into me with the same percussive force as some of hers.

"If you touch one of those poles, you'll die..."

—Perhaps she didn't say it exactly in those terms...

—Perhaps not... but that was how it reached me. If you touch that, you'll die...
We are going for a walk somewhere in the country, I don't remember where, Mama is walking slowly, on Kolya's

arm... I am behind, rooted to the spot in front of the wooden telegraph pole... "If you touch that, you'll die," Mama said that... I have an urge to touch it, I want to know, I'm very frightened, I want to see what it will be like, I stretch out my hand, I touch the wood of the telegraph pole with my finger... and, immediately, that's it, it's happened to me, Mama knew it, Mama knows everything, it's certain, I'm dead, I run up to them screaming, I hide my head in Mama's skirts, I shout with all my strength: I'm dead... they don't know it, I'm dead... But what's the matter with you? I'm dead, dead, dead, I touched the pole, there, it's happened, the horrible thing, the most horrible thing possible was in that pole, I touched it and it passed into me, it's in me, I roll on the ground to get it to come out, I sob, I howl, I'm dead... they pick me up in their arms, they shake me, kiss me... No, no, you're quite all right... I touched the pole, Mama told me... she laughs, they both laugh, and this calms me...

"Here, Mama, please, eat this..." Mama, who isn't wearing her pince-nez, she only wears it for reading, bends down very low to see what is in the spoon I'm holding up to her... "It's dust I've collected for you, it isn't a bit dirty, don't be afraid, eat it... You already have..."

"What on earth are you talking about? You're crazy..."

"No. You told me that that was how I grew in your stomach... because you'd eaten some dust... eat this too, oh, please do, do it for me, I would so like to have a sister or a brother..."

Mama looks slightly irritated... "I don't know what I told you..."

"You told me *that*. And you also said, I heard you... you said you would like to have another child... So do it, Mama, here, eat it..."

Mama pushes down my outstretched hand... "But it

wasn't that sort of dust..."

"Tell me, then... *what* sort of dust?"

"Oh, I don't know..."

"Yes, you do. Tell me..."

"It was the sort of dust there is on flowers..."

"On flowers? On which flowers?"

"I've forgotten."

"Make an effort, though, try and remember..."

"Oh, listen, stop plaguing me with your questions. You'd do better to go and play, like all the other children, instead of trailing around behind me with nothing to do, you just don't know what to think up next, you can see very well that I'm busy..."

I am sitting beside Mama in a closed carriage drawn by one horse, we are bumping over a dusty road. I'm holding a French children's book as close as possible to the window and trying to read it in spite of the jolts, in spite of Mama's rebukes: "Stop it, now, that's quite enough, you'll ruin your eyes..."

The town we are going to is called Kamenetz-Podolsk. We are going to spend the summer there with my Uncle Grisha Shatunowsky, one of my mother's brothers, who is a barrister.

What we are going towards, what is in store for me there, has all the qualities of the events that make for "happy childhood memories"... of those that their possessors usually exhibit with a touch of pride. And how could one not feel proud of having had parents who took the trouble to prepare the ground for you to have memories which conform in every detail to the most valued, the most highly thought-of models? I must confess that I am a little hesitant...

—That's understandable... a beauty that conforms so closely to the models... But after all, when for once you, too, are lucky enough to possess such memories, you can let yourself go a little, what does it matter, it's so tempting...

—But they weren't made for me, they were just lent to me, I was only able to enjoy them piecemeal...

—That may be what made them more intense... No danger of them losing their flavour... No getting into the habit...

—Oh, no, no chance of that. Everything retained its exquisite perfection: the huge family house full of nooks and crannies, little staircases... the "hall," as they were called in the houses of old Russia, with a big grand piano, mirrors everywhere, gleaming parquet floors, and all along the walls, chairs swathed in white dust covers... The long dining room table where, at either end, facing each other, talking to each other from a distance, smiling at each other, the father and mother sit between their four children, two boys and two girls... After the dessert, when my aunt has given the children permission to leave the table, they go up to their parents to thank them, they kiss their hands and receive a kiss on the head, on the cheek... I like taking part in this amusing ceremony...

The servants, as is right and proper, are pleasantly familiar and devoted... Nothing is lacking... even the old *nyanya*, soft and sweet in her shawl and her ample skirts... for our tea she gives us succulent slices of white bread spread with a thick layer of moistened sugar... and the coachman, sunning himself on the wooden bench against the little wall in the courtyard where the stables are... I like to climb quietly up on to the wall behind him and put my hands over his eyes... "Guess who it is..." "I know it's you, you little rascal..." I cling on to his broad back, I put my arms round his neck, I breathe in the delightful odour exuding from his leather waistcoat, his ample jacket, his pomaded hair, the sweat forming in fine droplets on his tanned, craggy skin...

And the garden... with, at its far end, the meadow covered in tall grasses where we always go to play—Lola, the youngest of my girl cousins, who is my age, her brother Petya, and some neighbours' or friends' children... We crush between our thumb and index finger the empty, yellowish husks, of I don't remember what plant, so as to hear them burst, we squeeze a flattened, sharp-edged blade of grass between our two thumbs and blow on it, to make it start whistling... With my head covered in a long white muslin veil and encircled by a crown of daisies that Nyanya has woven, holding a beautifully smooth wand, still a little moist, a little greenish, and fragrant with the scent of freshly stripped wood, I lead the procession which is going to consign to earth a big, black, flat watermelon seed. It reposes in a little box on a layer of moss... we bury it according to the gardener's instructions, we water it with our children's little watering can, I wave my magic wand over the earth, pronouncing incantations composed of amusing, barbaric syllables which I remembered for a long time but can no longer call to mind... We shall go and inspect this tomb until the day when we may perhaps be lucky enough to see a tender, living shoot come out of the earth... At the bottom of the well, a very small but very dangerous monster lives under its carapace, its sting is mortal, if it comes out and makes its way along the path, we may not see it, its colour merges into the colour of the sand...

Of my uncle's face, all that I retain is an impression of fine features, of rather sad kindliness... we see very little of him, mostly at meals... he works so hard.

On the other hand, I can see my aunt very clearly, as she appeared to me when I liked to look at her silvery curls, her pink complexion, her eyes... the only blue eyes I have ever seen with a truly violet tinge... even that gap between her two very white, very slightly protruding front teeth adds to her charm. There is something in her gaze, in the way she carries her head, which gives her a certain air... the only word I can find to describe it today is regal... Mama says that Aunt Anyiuta is "a real beauty."

She is holding a big round watch in her hand, she places one finger of her other hand on its dial and asks me: "If the big hand is there and the little one there... You don't know? Think carefully... don't prompt her, Lola..." I think as hard as I can, I'm afraid I shall be wrong, I murmur a hesitant answer, and she gives me a big smile, she exclaims: "Good! Very good!"

We are sitting with her, we, the youngest children, in the big open barouche drawn by two horses, we are going to the other side of the river, where the shops are, and where there is the tall white tower with a balcony running round it near the top... Even from a distance, from our bank, we can see a silhouette leaning over the balustrade, it's emitting strange sounds which are like calls, like songs. Our barouche fords the wide river, the water comes up higher than the footboard, almost covers the horses' ribs, but we mustn't be frightened, nothing can happen to us, the coachman knows his way very well... and here we are at last on dry land, the horses climb up the opposite bank, we trot along the white road towards the pâtisserie, the bookshops, the toyshops, the shoeshops... my aunt examines the shoes I have on my feet, already the worse for wear, soon too small... You, too, you need new ones...

In my aunt's very bright, blue and white bedroom, there are all sorts of little bottles on the dressing table. They contain perfumes, eau de Cologne. Here is an empty one which she is going to throw into the wastepaper basket, but I stop her... "Oh, please, don't throw it away, give it to me..."

Here we are, the little bottle and I, alone in my bedroom. I turn it round cautiously in all directions, the better to see its curved lines, its smooth surfaces, its oval, faceted stopper... We shall start by removing everything that disfigures you... in the first place, this horrid ribbon knotted round your neck... and then, there, on the front, that thick yellow shiny label... I lift one corner of it and pull... it comes off easily, but leaves in its place a dry, hard, whitish patch, which I soften by moistening it with a little rag or piece of cotton wool soaked in the water from the pitcher, and it comes off in thin shreds which roll up under my finger... but it hasn't all gone, there's still a fine deposit which has to be scraped off with a penknife, being careful not to scratch the glass... And now everything that detracts from its beauty has been removed, the bottle is naked and ready for its toilet. I fill it with water, I shake it to empty it properly, so that it no longer has the slightest trace of what it used to contain, I soap it and then rinse it in the wash basin. Next, I dry it with my towel, and when it is quite dry, I set about making it gleam by polishing it with a corner of my blanket or with one of my woollen garments. Then it appears in all its dazzling purity... I hold it up to the window to exhibit it to the light, I take it out into the garden so that it can sparkle in the sun... in the evenings, I gaze at it under the lamp... Nothing threatens us, no one will come and take it away from me, Lola is only interested in her dolls, Petya gives it a vacant stare...

I have several of them now, all different, but each is splendid in its own way.

A collection lined up on my mantelpiece, which no one but me—they have promised—is allowed to touch.

When I take one out with me, I keep it wrapped up, I don't want any frivolous looks or remarks to reach it.

—It's strange that your passion for those little bottles should have disappeared as soon as you left.

—That's true, I didn't take any of them with me. Perhaps

because I had stopped playing with them all the time I was ill... one of those minor, but contagious illnesses... was it Chicken Pox? German measles? In my bedroom, slightly darkened by a big tree, with a communicating door to Mama's room, I'm lying in my little bed against the far wall, I realize that I have a high temperature by the presence... they are always there when my body, my head, are burning... of little gnomes perpetually emptying bags of sand, the sand runs out, spreads everywhere, they empty more and more, I don't know why these piles of sand and the agitation of the little gnomes frighten me so much, I try to stop them, I try to shout out, but they don't hear me, I can't manage to shout properly.

When my temperature has gone down, I can sit up in my bed... A chambermaid sent by my aunt cleans the room, makes my bed, washes me, does my hair, gives me something to drink, to eat...

Mama is there too, but I can only see her sitting at the table, writing on enormous white pages, which she numbers with huge figures, which she covers with her big writing, which she throws on the floor when she has filled them. Or else Mama is in an armchair, reading...

—Be fair, she did sometimes, during this illness, come and sit by your bed with a book.

—That's true, and not with one of her books, with one of my books... I can see it now, I knew it well... it was a children's edition of *Uncle Tom's Cabin*. A big bound book, with greyish illustrations. In one of them you could see Eliza jumping from one block of ice to the next with her

child in her arms. In another, Uncle Tom dying, and opposite, on the other page, the description of his death. Both
pages were slightly puckered, some of the letters were obliterated... they had so often been soaked by my tears...

Mama reads to me in her deep voice, without putting in
any expression... the words come out brisk and clear... at
moments I have the impression that she isn't giving much
thought to what she is reading... when I tell her that I'm
sleepy or that I'm tired, she shuts the book very quickly, I
feel she's glad to stop...

—Did you really feel that at that moment?

—I think so, I perceived it, but I didn't judge her in any
way... wasn't it natural that a children's book would not
interest a grown-up who likes to read difficult books? It was
only at the end, when I got up, when I was about to go
down into the garden...

—This is the end of the "happy memories" which you
had such scruples about... they conformed too closely to
the model...

—Yes... it didn't take long for them to regain the privilege
of conforming to nothing but themselves... Standing in my
room, still not very steady on my feet, through the open
door I heard Mama saying to I don't know whom: "When I
think that I have stayed shut up here with Natasha all this
time without anyone dreaming of taking my place with

her." But what I felt at that moment had soon vanished...

—Had sunk, perhaps, but...

—Probably... but in any case it had sunk deep enough for me not to see anything on the surface. One gesture, one affectionate word from Mama was enough, or even just seeing her, sitting in her armchair reading, raising her head, looking surprised when I go up and speak to her, she looks at me through her pince-nez, their lenses enlarging her bronze-coloured eyes, they seem immense, full of naiveté, innocence, good nature... and I cuddle up to her, I put my lips on the delicate, silky, soft skin of her forehead, of her cheeks.

As if in a break in a silvery mist, it is always this same road that emerges, covered in a thick blanket of very white snow, with no trace of footsteps or wheels, along which I am walking beside a fence that is taller than me, made of thin wooden planks with pointed tops...

—That's what I predicted: always the same image, unchanged, permanently engraved...

—True. And here's another, which always appears at the mere mention of the word Ivanovo... that of a long wooden house whose façade is punctuated by numerous windows surmounted, like lace fringes, by little awnings of carved wood... the enormous icicles hanging in clusters from its roof are sparkling in the sun... the courtyard in front of the house is covered in snow... Not a single detail changes from one time to the next. However hard I look, like in the game of "spot the errors," I can't discover the slightest modification.

—Ah, you see...

—Yes... but I can't resist it, I want to touch, to caress this immutable image, to cover it with words, but not too thickly, I'm so afraid of spoiling it... I want the words to come here too, to alight... in the interior of the house, in the big room with the very white walls... its gleaming parquet floor is strewn with coloured rugs... the divans, the armchairs, are covered in flowered cotton fabrics... big tubs contain all sorts of indoor plants... in the windows, between the double panes, there's a layer of white cotton wool sprinkled with silver spangles. No house in the world has ever seemed more beautiful to me than this house. A real Christmas story house... and, what's more, the house where I was born.

—And yet something stops it from figuring among those "happy childhood memories," which your uncle's house deserved.

—I know what it is: it's the absence of my mother. Never for a single instant does she appear there.

—She would have appeared if you were one of those people who have the gift of remembering their very earliest years... some people can almost remember things dating back to their birth...

—Yes, but I am not so lucky... I can remember nothing that happened before my departure from Ivanovo, at the age of two, nothing of the departure itself, nothing of my father, or of my mother, or of Kolya, with whom, as I later discovered, we left, she and I, first for Geneva, and then, for Paris.

But it isn't only my mother who is absent from that house. Out of all the people who must have been there when I went back for a few weeks from time to time, I can see no one but my father... his slim, upright silhouette, always seeming a little tense... He is sitting on the edge of a divan with me on his knees, I am looking at the tall windows completely veiled by a white curtain... He's teaching me to count them... is it possible? and yet I remember it distinctly... I count up to ten, plus one, the last one, which makes eleven...

I am standing in front of him between his parted legs, my shoulders are on a level with his knees... I am reciting the days of the week... Monday, Tuesday, Wednesday, Thursday, Friday, Saturday, Sunday... and then Monday, Tuesday... "That will do now, you know them..." "But what comes after that?" "After that, they start again..." "Always the same? But until when?" "Always." "But if I repeat it again and again? If I say it all day long? If I say it all night long? will they come back again, Monday, Tuesday, always?" "Always, my little idiot..." his hand gently caresses my head, I feel something radiating from him... something that he keeps locked inside him, that he keeps in check, he doesn't like to show it, but it's there, I feel it, it was conveyed by his hand, which he quickly withdrew, by his eyes, by his voice which pronounces those diminutives that only he makes out of my name: Tashok, or the diminutive of this diminutive: Tashotshek... and also the comic name he gives me: Pigalitza... when I ask him what that is, he tells me it's the name of a little bird.

I like to pass my hand over his thin, rather craggy cheeks, to squeeze their skin between my fingers and lift it up, to tickle the nape of his neck... he pushes me away gently... and also sometimes, when he isn't expecting it, to give him a big kiss in the hollow of his ear and see how it deafens him, he sticks a finger into it and wiggles it, shaking his head... pretends to be angry... "What a stupid game..."

He often speaks French with me... I think he speaks it perfectly, it's just that he rolls his "r"s... I try to teach him... Listen when I say Paris... listen carefully, Paris... and now say it like I do... Paris... *no*, that's not it... he imitates me comically, purposely exaggerating, as if he were hurting his throat... Parrris... He gets his own back when he teaches me to pronounce the Russian "r" properly, I must curl up the tip of my tongue and press it against my palate, then uncurl it... but however hard I try... Ah, you see, now you're the one who can't do it... and we laugh, we love to make fun of each other in this way...

My father is the only one who remains present everywhere. It seems to me now that the objects around us are manipulated by invisible beings.

A spoon going round the edge of my plate where it isn't so hot, cautiously scoops up some of the delicious semolina pudding spread out in a big circle... the spoon is lifted up to my mouth, for me to blow on...

A spoon filled with strawberry jam comes up to my lips... I turn my head away, I don't want any more... it tastes horrible, I don't recognize it... what has happened to it? something has crept into the lovely flavour it always has... something revolting is hiding in it... it makes me feel sick, "I don't like it, it isn't real strawberry jam." "But of course it is, you can see very well that it is..." Very carefully, I examine the thin layer of jam spread out over the saucer... the strawberries are certainly like the ones I know, they are only just a little paler, less red or dark pink, but on them, between them, there are sort of suspicious whitish streaks... "No, look, there's something in it..." "There's nothing at all, you're imagining it..." When my father comes back I tell him that I didn't want that jam... it's bad, I looked carefully, there were white streaks in it, little white spots, it tasted disgusting... It isn't strawberry jam... He observes me, he hesitates for a moment, then he says: "It *was* strawberry jam, but what you saw in it was a little calomel. They had mixed it into the jam, they hoped you wouldn't notice, I know you hate calomel, but you absolutely have to take it..."

The rather disturbing impression of something revolting being deceitfully smuggled in, hidden under the appearance of something delicious, has never faded, and even today, it sometimes comes back to me when I put a spoonful of strawberry jam in my mouth.

My father has had a little mound of thickly packed snow built for me in the courtyard in front of the house. I climb up its gentle slope and come down its steep slope on my toboggan... I climb up and come down again indefatigably, my face is burning, steam comes out of my nostrils, my mouth, my whole being breathes in the air of the winter frosts.

I have been given a big bound book, a very thin one, which I love looking through, I enjoy listening when they read me what is written opposite the pictures... but careful! —we're getting to *that* picture, it frightens me, it's horrible... a very thin man with a long, pointed nose, dressed in a bright green frock coat with floating tails, is brandishing a pair of open scissors, he's going to cut into the flesh, blood is going to flow... "I can't look at it, it must go..." "Would you like us to tear out the page?" "That would be a pity, it's such a beautiful book." "Well, then, we'll hide that picture... We'll stick the pages together." Now I don't see it any more, but I know that it's still there, shut in... here it is, approaching, hidden here, where the page gets thicker... I have to turn the pages very quickly, I have to pass over this one before it has time to alight in me, to become embedded... it has already begun to take shape, those scissors cutting into the flesh, those big drops of blood... but that's it now, we've passed it, it's eclipsed by the next picture.

In the illustrations of my favourite book, *Max and Moritz*, with its comic verses that I know by heart, that I love to chant, nothing ever frightens me, even when I see the two naughty little rascals tied to a dish, ready to be put into the oven and roasted like two little sucking pigs...

—Is it certain that that picture is in *Max and Moritz*? Wouldn't it be better to check?

—No, what's the point? What *is* certain is that that picture is still associated with this book and that the feeling it gave me has remained intact: a feeling of apprehension, of a kind of fear which wasn't real fear, but just a funny sort of fear that you could enjoy.

They take the brown wrapping paper off a big cardboard box, they remove its lid, its tissue paper, and a huge doll with closed eyes is revealed, lying there... she has brown curls, her eyelids are framed in long, thick lashes... she's the one, I recognize her, she's the one I had seen in Paris in a big, brightly lit shop window, I had looked so hard at her... She was sitting in an armchair, and at her feet was a card on which was written: "I can talk"... They take her out very carefully... when they lift her up her eyes open... when she turns her head, this way or that, there is a sound in her... "Do you hear? she talks, she says Papa Mama..." "Yes, that's what she seems to be saying... but what else can she say?" "She's too little, it's quite an achievement for her to be able to say that... Don't be afraid, though, take her in your arms."

I pick her up very carefully and put her on the divan, to see her better... There's no denying it, she is very beautiful... she is wearing a white tulle dress, a blue satin sash, blue shoes and socks, and a big blue ribbon in her hair... "Can she be undressed?"... "Of course... and we can even make her some other clothes... then you'll be able to change her, you can dress her however you like..." Yes, I'm pleased, I give Papa a big kiss. "She *was* the one you wanted, then?" "Yes, she's the one..." They leave us alone together so we can get to know each other better. I stay by her side, I lay her down, I sit her up, I make her turn her head and say Papa Mama. But I don't feel very much at my ease with her. And time doesn't improve matters, I never feel like playing with her... She's too hard, too smooth, she always makes the same movements, you can only make her move by raising or lowering, always in the same way, her slightly bent arms and legs, jointed to her stiff body. I much prefer the old bran dolls I have had for ages, it isn't that I am so fond of them, but you can treat their rather flabby, disjointed bodies in any way you like, hug them, mess them about, throw them...

Mishka is the only one who is really close to me, Mishka, my teddy bear, silky, warm, soft, cuddly, completely imbued with tender familiarity. He always sleeps with me, his head with its golden fur, its perky ears, lies by my side on the pillow, his nice round nose, as black as his bright little eyes, stick out above the sheet... I couldn't go to sleep if I didn't feel him there by my side, I never go away without him, he accompanies me on all my journeys.

I have been taken to fetch Papa from his "factory" where he works all day long... I cross a big, muddy courtyard and then go past a group of huts on the tamped earth, I have to jump over streams, pools of blue, yellow, red liquid... among the casks, the carts, bearded men wearing caps and tall boots are moving around... the smell here isn't as disgusting as the smell of vinegar, but I try to breathe it in as little as possible, it is so disagreeable, acrid, acid... I go into a long, very brightly lit room, where there are several long tables on which you can see, standing side by side in wooden supports, test tubes containing powders of the same dazzling colour as the streams in the courtyard, reds, blues, yellows... liquids of the same lovely colour are being heated in retorts suspended above little flames... Papa is standing in front of one of the tables, wearing long white overalls, he's holding a retort, he shakes it gently over the flame and then raises it and examines it in the light. He puts it back in its stand, bends down, picks me up in his arms, kisses me, and then takes me into an adjoining room, where he perches me on some big books, in his armchair, at his desk. He pushes a big abacus towards me and says...

"Here, play with this... I shan't be long." I slide, pull down, push up the yellow and black wooden balls along the metal rods they are threaded on, but it isn't much fun, I don't know how to play with them... I can't wait until Papa comes back... then, here he is, he has taken off his overalls, he's wearing his black pelisse and his fur hat, he looks pleased... "There, you see, it wasn't very long."

Here he is, in a vast, snow-covered square, I know it's a square in Moscow, he comes out of a big confectioner's shop, his arms laden with parcels wrapped in white paper, tied with ribbons... I love to see him like that... the otter-skin collar of his black pelisse casually open, showing his high white collar, his fur hat pushed back a little... he is smiling, I don't know why... on his animated face, from which something even more intense than usual is radiating, there is the gleam of the flawless, regular, very white line of his teeth.

He comes up to the sledge in which, muffled up to the eyes, protected by the leather apron, I am waiting for him... he unfastens the apron on one side only, deposits the parcels under my feet and slides in by my side behind the enormous back of the coachman dressed in his thick box coat.

We are in my father's flat in Moscow. There is a big Christmas tree in the middle of one of the rooms. This time I can vaguely discern a pretty young blonde woman who likes to laugh and to play... I hand her all sorts of little parcels, objects, toys, which are on the floor under the tree, golden nuts, tiny, little red apples from the Crimea, and she ties them on to the branches with red ribbons, gold and silver thread...

And then, in the entrance hall, the children are sitting, our guests who are leaving after the party... they have their shoes taken off, the grown-ups look everywhere, under the benches, then find, and put on their outstretched legs, their felt boots.

I am lying in my little room that has been prepared for me in this same flat, my bed is against a wall covered with a straw mat with embroidered designs. I always lie facing it, I like to stroke its smooth texture with my finger, to look at its delicate golden colour, the silky sparkle of its birds, its shrubs, its flowers... Here, I don't know why, I'm afraid when I'm alone in my room in the evenings, and Papa has agreed to stay with me until I fall asleep... He is sitting on a chair behind me and singing me an old lullaby... his bass voice is uncertain, sort of slightly husky... he doesn't sing very well, and this awkwardness makes what he sings even more touching... I can hear him so distinctly today that I can imitate him, and I admit that I sometimes do so... in that lullaby, he has replaced the words "my baby" by the diminutive of my name, which has the same number of syllables, Tashotshek... I gradually begin to doze off, his voice becomes farther and farther away... and then I hear behind me the faint sound of his chair, he must be standing up, he thinks I'm asleep, he's going to leave... and at once I lift a hand out from under the blanket to show him that I am still awake... or I hear the parquet floor creaking under his slow, prudent footsteps... he's going to half-open the door very quietly... so I give a little cough, a little grunt... but I don't speak, that might wake me up completely and I want to go to sleep, I want him to be able to go, I don't like making him stay...

—Really? Don't you rather think that when you felt him behind your back, his eyes riveted on you, singing under his breath more and more softly, tiptoeing towards the door, looking back one last time from the threshold to observe you, to make sure that you haven't suspected anything, and then, opening the door, shutting it again with immense precaution and, finally, free at last, making his escape... don't you rather think that what made you lift your hand, cough, grunt, was the desire to prevent what was in the air, what was about to happen, and which for you already smacked of veiled treachery, of abandon?

—I agree that all the signs seemed to be combined to make that occur to me... But I'm trying to feel myself back there, in that little bed, listening to my father standing up, walking over to the door... I lift my hand, I give a little grunt... no, not yet, don't go, I shall be frightened, you promised me, we agreed that you would stay with me until I fell asleep, I'm doing my best, I shall manage, you'll see, I mustn't speak, I mustn't move too much, I simply want to show you, since we agreed, since there was a pact between us, I know you want to respect it, and I do, too, you know, I do respect it, I'm just showing you... you don't want me to be frightened... stay just a little bit longer, I can feel that I'm nearly asleep, then everything will be all right for me, I won't feel anything any more, and you can be quite happy to leave me, to go away...

The barouche stops at the steps leading up to a big wooden house, Papa extricates me from the covers I am bundled up in, he takes me in his arms, I am very little, I'm wearing my white velvet coat, which is so beautiful that people tell me that I'm a "real doll" in it, he dashes up the steps, carrying me, he puts me in the arms of my grand-father and grandmother, who are both standing there by the door, in their long white nightgowns... Papa speaks to them furiously... "But I told you, I asked you not to get up, it's madness..."

I am so shocked that he should speak to them in this manner that I am petrified, I don't respond as I would like to their kisses, to their affectionate words... *They* don't seem to resent Papa's manner... Perhaps they are too weak to stand up for themselves, they are so gentle, so old... How could he have been so angry, have spoken so roughly to them? The moment we are alone I ask him... "You seemed so unkind..." "Of course not, don't be silly, I was afraid they would catch cold... at seven in the morning! in their nightgowns! They could have waited in their bed, I'd writ-ten to them..." "But you didn't have to say it so unkindly..." "But I didn't, it wasn't unkind..." "You shouted..." "To get them to go in quickly, they're hard of hearing... I didn't want them to catch cold..." "Do they know that that was why?" "Of course they know. You'd do better to think about something else..."

And I really would have done better. Then I might perhaps have remembered other moments of this unique visit to my grandparents... but it seems that that particular moment, which was so violent, immediately overpowered all the others, it is the only one that has remained.

I am going for a walk with my father... or rather, he is taking me for a walk, as he does every day when he comes to Paris. I don't remember how our rendezvous was arranged... someone must have taken me to his hotel or to some pre-arranged meeting place... it is out of the question for him to come and fetch me at the rue Flatters... I have never seen them, I can't imagine them together, him and my mother...

We have gone into the Grand Luxembourg gardens, through the main gate opposite the Senate, and we are making our way over to the left, towards the puppet show, the swings, the merry-go-round...

Everything is grey, the air, the sky, the paths, the vast, barren spaces, the leafless branches on the trees. I rather think we were silent. At all events, the only thing I remember of what may have been said are these words, which I can still hear very distinctly: "Do you love me, Papa?..." with no anxiety in my tone, but something that was intended to be mischievous... it isn't possible for me to ask this question seriously, for me to say "do you love me" in any other way than as a joke... he hates words of that sort too much, and in the mouth of a child...

—Did you really already feel that, at that age?

—Yes, just as intensely as I would have felt it now, perhaps even more so... these are things that children perceive much better than adults do.

I knew that the words "you love me," " I love you," were among those that would make him wince, would make something buried inside him retreat, become even more deeply embedded... And, indeed, there is disapproval in his expression, in his voice... "Why do you ask me that?" Still with a touch of amusement in my tone ... because this does amuse me, but also to prevent him rebuffing me in displeasure, "Don't talk nonsense"... I insist: "Do you love me, tell me." "But you know I do..." "But I'd like you to say it. Say it, Papa, do you love me or not?"... this time in a minatory, solemn tone of voice which allows him to sense what is coming next and incites him... it's only a game, it's only for fun... which incites him to let out these ridiculous, indecent words: "Of course I do, my silly little goose, *I love you.*"

Then he is rewarded for having agreed to play my game... "Well then, since you love me, you're going to give me..." You see, I didn't for a moment dream of obliging you to lay yourself bare, to disclose what you are filled with, what you hold back, what you only ever allow to escape in dribs and drabs, you might have let it trickle out just a little bit... "You're going to give me one of those balloons..." "But where do you see them?" "Over there... there are some in that kiosk..."

And I am satisfied, I've been able to tease him a little and then to reassure him... and to receive this pledge, this pretty trophy, which I carry off, floating all blue and sparkling above my head, attached to a long string tied round my wrist.

I'm big enough now not to have to be put in a carriage, I can sit astride that yellow lion, or rather, that pink pig... or else, no, that beautiful white giraffe... With my left hand, I grip the copper shaft to which I am attached by a belt round my waist, and in my right hand, I hold the smooth, round wooden handle with the long metal rod...

The music starts to play, we are off... you have to be very careful to hold the metal rod at the right angle, we're revolving, in a few seconds we shall be passing the ring... and here it is, suspended in the air, swaying gently... it's coming closer... I'm getting very near to it, this is the moment... I hold the rod out towards it, I aim straight ahead, right in its center... got it, I hear a metallic noise, but it's only the sound it made when it knocked against the rod, it didn't hook it and it's already behind me, we go on revolving... never mind, I shall start again... And the next time round, once again...

—Try to remember, though... you must sometimes have...

—Yes, certainly, since I remember those two or three rings

I deposited on the counter on my way out... But what is that, when other children as little as me, and even littler, are so good at hooking them... at the end of the trip the rings they have managed to thread on the rod almost entirely cover it... Nevertheless, I take the stick of barley sugar that they give me, I listen to the consolation and advice of the grown-ups... "You see, you get too tense, you mustn't, you saw how the other children do it... they do it for fun..." Yes, I would so much like to be able, like them, with their ease, their lightheartedness, their insouciance... Why can't I? After all, what does it matter?... it's true, why should it be important?... But perhaps the next time... if I go about it the right way...

When, from a distance, I catch sight of the green railings round the merry-go-round and see its multicoloured shapes gliding, revolving, when I hear its jerky music, I want to run up to it, I want us to hurry... "Do you really want a ride?" "Oh yes, I *do*."

"Dearest little pillow, with choicest feathers sewn, so soft and warm beneath my head, and made for me alone..." as I recite, I can hear my little voice, which I am making shriller than it really is because I want it to be the voice of a very little girl, and I can also hear the affected silliness of my intonation... I am perfectly well aware of how false, how ridiculous is this imitation of the innocence, the naiveté of a little child, but it's too late, I've let myself in for it, I didn't dare resist when they picked me up under my arms and stood me on that chair so that they could see me better... if they left me on the floor, they wouldn't be able to see me properly, my head would hardly reach above the long table where, on either side of a bride dressed all in white, people are sitting, looking at me, waiting... I have been pushed, I have fallen, into this voice, this tone, I can't retreat, I have to advance, masquerading under this disguise of a baby, a silly goose, and now I've come to the place where I have to feign terror, I part my lips, I open my eyes wide, my voice rises, vibrates... "When you're afraid of the wolf, of the wind, of the storm..." and then, the tender, naive emotion... "Dearest little pillow, how well I sleep on you..." I follow it through to the bitter end, this path of submission, of abject renunciation of everything I feel myself to be, of everything I really am, my cheeks are burning, while they lift me down from my chair, while of my own accord I make the little curtsey of the well-brought up, good little girl and run off to hide... in whose lap?... what was I doing there?... who had taken me there?... to the approving laughs, the amused, sympathetic exclamations, the loud clapping...

One more name which, curiously enough, has remained: the rue Boissonade. It was there, in a big, light, ground-floor room, that I had come, I don't remember how, to meet Papa... He is sitting, always slim and upright, on a settee, and I am sitting by his side... A door opens in the wall opposite us and a young woman enters... I have seen her before, it isn't the Moscow one who decorated the Christmas tree with me, but a different one, with dark brown hair, whom I have only seen here, with Papa... she makes her entrance disguised as a young man... she is wearing one of Papa's suits, and on her head she has his bowler hat, under which she has concealed her bun, but there are little curls hanging down over her cheeks, over the nape of her neck... her eyes are a very light blue and seem to be transparent... we look at her, surprised, we laugh, isn't she funny, dressed up like that, doesn't it suit her... she comes up to me, she bows to me like they do to ladies at balls, she takes my hand, I stand up, she holds me about the waist and whirls round with me humming charming merry stirring tunes she goes faster and faster she lifts me up my feet aren't touching the ground any more my head is swimming I laugh in delight... finally, she takes me back to the divan, lets go of me, drops me, lets herself drop down beside Papa and me, her bosom heaves, her cheeks, round like children's cheeks, are all pink, she throws her head against the back of the divan and fans herself with her handkerchief, still panting a little, smiling... How I wish she would start again.

Why try to bring this back to life, without the words that might manage to capture, to retain, if only for a few more instants, what happened to me... as celestial visions appear to little shepherd girls... but here there is no saintly apparition, no pious child...

I was sitting, again in the Luxembourg gardens, on a bench in the English garden, between my father and the young woman who had danced with me in the big, light room in the rue Boissonade. On the bench between us, or on the knees of one of them, there was a big, bound book... I rather think it was Hans Andersen's *Fairy Tales*.

I had just been listening to a passage from it... I was looking at the blossom on the espaliers along the little pink brick wall, the trees in bloom, the sparkling green lawn strewn with pink and white petaled daisies, the sky, of course, was blue, and the air seemed to be gently vibrating... and at that moment, it happened... something unique... something that will never again happen in that way, a sensation of such violence that, even now, after so much time has elapsed, when it comes back to me, faded and partially obliterated, I feel... but what? what word can pin it down? not the all-encompassing word: "happiness," which is the first that comes to mind, no, not that... "felicity," "exaltation," are too ugly, they mustn't touch it... and "ecstasy"... at this word, everything in it recoils... "Joy," yes, perhaps... this modest, very simple little word may alight on it with no great danger... but it cannot gather up what fills me, brims over in me, disperses, dissolves, melts into the pink bricks, the blossom-covered espaliers, the lawn, the pink and white petals, the air vibrating with barely perceptible tremors, with waves... waves of life, quite simply of life, what other word?... of life in its pure state, no lurking menace, no mixture, it suddenly attains the greatest intensity it can ever attain... never again that kind of intensity, for no reason, just because it is there, because I am inside it, inside the little pink wall, the flowers on the espaliers, on the trees, the lawn, the vibrating air... I am inside them with nothing else, nothing that does not belong to them, nothing that belongs to me.

It is in this wide street, lined on one side with light-coloured houses and on the other with gardens, so different from the rue Flatters, that Mama and Kolya now live.

In the entrance hall and on the stairs, there is a thick red carpet, and in the left-hand wall, a lift, like in hotels. And also, as in hotels, a concierge dressed in a beautiful tail coat trimmed with braid and wearing a top hat... he helps to take up my luggage.

I go into a big, light room, where Mama and Kolya kiss me, step back a little so as to see me better... "But you look wonderful, how you've grown... and what a pretty coat you're wearing... turn round, let us look at you..." It is indeed very pretty, dark blue, with a blue velvet collar and trimmings, and I am wearing my kid gloves... Papa, squatting in front of me on the pavement, by the door of a shop, in Paris, had had a lot of trouble fitting them over my fingers, which I held stiff and outspread, but the gloves stretched, as the salesgirl had promised, and now the press stud fastens easily without pinching, without creasing my skin at the wrist.

The bedroom on the right-hand side of the big room is going to be mine. The bed and the little table beside it are at the far end, facing the window. The landscape stretching out behind the double windows here looks as if it is composed of vast, icy expanses... not of snow sparkling in the sun, as in Ivanovo, nor of sombre little squeezed-up houses, as in Paris... but everywhere of transparent, bluish ice. And the light here is a silvery grey. The town I have come to is called St. Petersburg.

The maid who looks after me here is very young, everything on her face is pale, her skin, her lips, her eyes, and it is very kind. She is called Gasha. She takes me for a walk every day, either in a nearby square or in a vast garden which I never see again, even now, other than with frost-covered trees and lawns encrusted with a layer of ice shining in that silvery light...

We also enjoy walking in the wide avenue that our street leads into, and looking in the shop windows. Here, they have a dark brown frame round them, and there is something a little clumsy, a little uncouth about the big letters painted in white on the glass... In almost every building, there is a very steep staircase leading down to a basement in which there is often a boutique or a café.

Gasha and I like to stop and gaze into the window of a shoe shop, she looks at high-heeled, black patent leather shoes, they are very beautiful, she's right, and I look at children's black patent leather ones with heels just a little higher than mine, almost like those of the grown-ups...

Often in the evenings, when my parents have gone out,

we play a game I have been given here: "The Writers' Quartet." It is very like the game of "Happy Families" I played in Paris. As you need four people to play it, Gasha and the other maid... all I remember of her is her presence... invite one of their friends who works in the same building.

On each white card, there is the portrait of a writer, under which is his name in red letters. Under that, printed in black, the titles of four of his works. My partners and I can read, and this game fascinates us.

We are sitting round the square table in the middle of the kitchen, which is lit by an oil lamp suspended from the ceiling, the walls are dark, always oozing a little. The dark brown surface of one of the doors sometimes seems to be moving, it oscillates slightly... at first this frightened me, but they explained that it was only the movements of the cockroaches swarming all over that door... little insects that don't bite and that are going to stay there... Nobody bothers about them, and they soon give me the impression, as they do everyone else, that they are part of the house. It's pleasant, it's nice and warm in this kitchen.

We deal the cards, we throw dice to see who is going to begin, and then the one that fate has chosen says to one of the others: "Give me Turgenev: *Fathers and Sons*." The other holds out her card. "And now..." in more confident tones... "you're going to give me Turgenev again: *A Sportsman's Sketches*..." Triumphant tone: "I haven't got it. So you, Gasha, can give me Tolstoy: *Anna Karenina*. Thank you. And you, Natasha: *The Kreutzer Sonata*. Thank you. And now give me..." "I haven't got it... so you can give me back..." and so on, from setbacks to victories... only the arrival of my parents stops us... Mama scolds us gently, she likes playing this game, she understands us... "But this is folly, it's midnight, what are you going to look like..." "But

I can get up late tomorrow."

—That's true, when you come to think of it, why didn't you go to school, as you did in Paris?

—I don't know. I have a vague recollection of a very gay classroom, with plenty of indoor plants, where I went for a short time, and of a fat little girl who had a very funny name, a combination of the word bee and the word honey... And also of their teaching us to write with the left hand as well as with the right hand. I had told Papa about this in a letter. And he had answered that it was a pure waste of time. I didn't go to that school any more, or to any other.

—Why not?

—I really can't imagine... Perhaps so that they didn't seem to be giving in to my father on that point. But such a suspicion never crossed my mind at the time. As I think I have already observed: I didn't ask myself that sort of question.

And for me, my mother, just like my father, was always beyond suspicion.

I felt, radiating from Kolya, from his round cheeks, his near-sighted eyes, his chubby hands, kindliness, good nature... I liked the air of admiration, almost of adoration, he sometimes had when he looked at Mama, the benevolent way he looked at me, his laugh, which was so easily aroused. When, in a discussion with Mama, he wanted to show his disagreement, he always, in a gently impatient tone of voice, used the same words: "Oh, don't say that, please"... or: "That isn't it at all, it's nothing of the sort"... never with any real displeasure, never the slightest shadow of aggression. I didn't understand much of what they said, I think they most often talked about writers, about books... I sometimes recognized some of the ones in my "quartet."

That warm current, that radiation, that passed between Kolya and Mama—I, too, received some of it, like waves...

—Once, though... you remember...

—But that was what I felt a long time afterwards... you

know very well that at the moment...

—Oh, even at the moment... and the proof is that those words remained in you forever, words heard that one and only time... that old saying...

—Mama and Kolya were pretending to be wrestling, they were enjoying themselves and I wanted to join in, I took Mama's side, I put my arms round her, as if to defend her, and she pushed me away gently... "Let go... husband and wife are on the same side." And I backed away.

—As quickly as if she had pushed you violently...

—And yet, at that moment, what I felt was very mild... it was like the tinkle of a glass being gently tapped...

—You really believe that?

—It seemed to me at that moment that Mama had thought that I was trying to defend her in earnest, that I believed she was being threatened and she wanted to reassure me... Let go... don't be frightened, nothing can happen to me... "Husband and wife are on the same side."

—And that was all? You didn't feel anything else? But

look... Mama and Kolya are arguing, getting worked up, they're pretending to be fighting, they're laughing, and you go up, you put your arms round your mother's skirt, and she frees herself... "Let go, husband and wife are on the same side"... seeming slightly irritated...

—That's right... I was disturbing their game.

—Come on, make an effort...

—I was interfering... intruding where I had no right to be.

—Good, go on...

—I was a foreign body... who was in the way...

—Yes: a foreign body. You couldn't have put it better. That's what you felt then, and with such force... A foreign body... Sooner or later, the organism it has infiltrated will eliminate it...

—No, not that... I didn't think that...

—Not *think*, of course not, I'll grant you that... but it

appeared, indistinct, unreal... an unknown promontory which for a moment looms up out of the fog... and then, once again, a thick fog envelops it...

—No, you're going too far...

—Yes. I'm staying very near, and you know it.

On the other side of the frozen Neva, between the palaces with the white columns, their façades painted in delicate colours, there was a house entirely built out of the water which the intense cold had frozen: the ice house.

It sprang, to my interminable enchantment, from a little book...

—Very different, so they say, from the macabre *Ice House* you might have seen years later in an edition for adults.

—I could never look at *that* house... I wanted to preserve my own... It has remained just as it appeared to me then, nestling in the hollow of that town, in the heart of those winters, the condensation of their bluish transparencies, of their sparkle... Its walls of thick ice, its windowpanes made of a layer of very thin ice, its balconies, its columns, its statues, make you think of precious stones, they are the color of sapphires, of opals... Inside the house, all the furni-

66

ture, the tables, the chairs, the beds, the pillows, the blankets, the hangings, the rugs, all the little objects you find in real houses, all the crockery, and even the logs in the fireplaces, are made of ice.

At night countless candles burn in the ice candlesticks, candelabra, chandeliers, without melting them... the house has become translucid and seems to be ablaze inside... an incandescent block of ice...

It was the fantasy of a Tsar that had had it erected... a Tsar like the one who lives in the palace on the immense white esplanade... When Gasha speaks of him, her voice drops, as if imbued with veneration... It is difficult for me to imagine that he is the same as other men... even his body must be different... "Does he have to wash? Do they have to soap him?" "But of course..." "He can get dirty, then?" "Yes, only *he* likes to be clean..." "And does he, too, have this little hole here in the middle of his stomach? And does it sometimes happen to him too, that it itches?"

There is laughter all round me in the overheated kitchen where I am standing in a big wooden tub, while Gasha makes me turn in every direction, soaps me and rinses me.

—It was at about this time that another book, *The Prince and the Pauper*, came into your life—and never left it.

—I don't think there was any other book in my childhood that I lived in as I lived in that one.

—Not even when you were *David Copperfield*, or the hero of Hector Malot's *No Relations*?

—No, not even those. Their lives were mine, as they were the lives of so many other children, but they didn't leave those furrows in me... two furrows which two images, and those two alone, ploughed...

That of the ragged little prince, perched on a barrel, crowned with a tin basin, an iron rod in his hand... and in a ring round him, in a red light... the light of hell itself... human beings with hideous bodies, sinister faces... He protests, he shouts out that he is Edward, the crown prince, their future king, that there's no doubt about it, that it's true... And they burst out laughing, they guffaw, they shout abuse at him, they pretend to be worshipping him, they entreat him, they kneel at his feet as a joke, they bow and scrape to him in a grotesque manner...

And then the image of Tom, the little pauper, the prince's double, dressed in his clothes, shut into the king's palace in his place... He is alone, far away from his family, surrounded by people he doesn't know, servants, solemn nobles, their faces are impenetrable, their eyes, covered with a thick film of respect, are staring at him... They observe his every gesture with veiled anxiety... Now one of them comes up to him and presents him with a golden bowl of water in which rose petals are floating... Tom hesitates, what is he supposed to do? finally, he makes his decision: he takes it in his hands, raises it and puts it to his lips... the finger bowl...

It is curious that, although I read this book over and over again, everything about it should have vanished except for these images, which still remain as intense, as intact.

I have almost too great a choice, there are books everywhere, in all the rooms, on the furniture and even on the floor, they have either been brought home by Mama and Kolya or come by post... small ones, middle-sized ones and big ones...

I inspect the newcomers, I gauge the effort each one is going to demand, how long it will take me... I choose one and settle down with it open on my knees, I grasp the wide paper knife made of greyish horn and I begin... First of all, the paper knife, held horizontally, separates the top of four pages bound together two by two, then it comes down, turns round, and slides between the two pages which are now joined only at the side... After that come the "easy" pages: their side is open, they only have to be separated at the top. And then again, the four "difficult" pages... then four "easy" pages, then four "difficult" ones, and so on, faster and faster, my hand gets tired, my head becomes heavy, it's buzzing, I feel a bit dizzy... "Stop now, my darling, that's enough, can't you really find anything more interesting to do? I'll cut it myself as I read, it doesn't bother me, I do it automatically..."

But there is no question of my abandoning it. All that I can allow myself, to reduce the boredom, to alleviate the dizziness, are a few variations: to start by doing only the "difficult" ones, leaving out the "easy" ones... and "saving them for dessert." Or else, on the contrary, to start with only the easy ones and finish with the difficult ones, or use one of these different methods on groups whose thickness I shall vary as I please... for example, three groups in which the difficult and the easy ones alternate... five in which I shall only start with the easy ones...

Once I have embarked on this business, I simply can't stop. I absolutely have to get to the moment when, with all its pages cut, the book becomes bigger, swollen, and I can shut it, press it to flatten it, and then, with my mind at rest, put it back in its place.

Mama insists, scolds me gently... "You shouldn't need so much persuading, it isn't nice, it isn't polite, go and fetch it, come and show it..." And the presence of the gentleman sitting by the window with his back to the light, his thoughtful silence, his expectation... all this weighs on me, incites me... but I know I mustn't do it, I shouldn't, I mustn't give in, I try my very hardest to resist... "But it's nothing at all, it was just to amuse myself... it's really nothing..." "Don't be so shy... you know that what she's writing is a whole long novel..." The gentleman...

—Who was he, I wonder?

—I find it impossible to remember. It could have been Korolenko, judging by the respect, the affection I felt Mama had for him... she wrote for his review, she saw a lot of him, Kolya and she often spoke of him... But his name doesn't matter. That respect, that affection, made the pressure of his words even more intense... irresistible... he spoke in exactly the same tone as he would use to a grown-up: "But it interests me very much. You must show it to me..." And then... to whom has this never happened? who can pretend to be unaware of the sensation we sometimes have when, knowing what is going to happen, what is in store for us, dreading it... we nevertheless let ourselves in for it...

—It's even almost as if we desire it, that that is what we are looking for...

—Yes, it draws you... a strange kind of attraction... I went to my room, I took from a drawer in my table a thick exercise book covered with black oilcloth, I brought it back and handed it to the gentleman...

—To "the uncle," you should say, since that's what children in Russia call adult men...

—Right. "The uncle" opens the exercise book at the first page... the letters are very clumsily written in red ink, the lines rise and fall... He glances over them rapidly, turns over a few more pages, stops from time to time... he looks amazed... he looks displeased... He shuts the exercise book, gives it back to me and says: "Anyone who sets out to write a *novel* should first learn to spell..."

—I took the exercise book back to my room, I don't remember what I did with it, in any case it disappeared, and I

73

didn't write another line...

—This is one of the rare moments of your childhood which you have occasionally, much later, spoken about...

—Yes, to reply, to give reasons to people who asked me why I waited so long before I began to "write"... It was so convenient, it would have been difficult to find anything more convincing: one of those magnificent "childhood traumas"...

—Did you really not believe in it?

—Yes, even so, I did believe in it... out of conformism. Out of laziness. You know very well how, until recently, I wasn't at all tempted to resuscitate the events of my childhood. But now, when I am making the effort to reconstitute those moments as best I can, what chiefly surprises me is that I can't recall having been at all angry, or having felt any resentment against "the uncle."

—It must have been there, though... He had been brutal...

—Certainly. But it probably disappeared very quickly, and what I *can* manage to recall is, above all, an impression of relief... rather like what one feels after having undergone an operation, cauterization, ablation... it was painful, but necessary, but beneficial...

—You couldn't possibly have realized that at the time...

—Of course not. It couldn't have appeared to me as I see it at present, now that I am obliging myself to make the effort... which I wasn't capable of... when I am trying to dig down, to reach, to grasp, to release what has remained there, buried.

I am in my bedroom, at my little table by the window. I am writing some words with my pen dipped in red ink... I can easily see that they aren't like real words in books... it's as if they are deformed, a bit crippled... Here is a very wobbly, unsteady one, I have to put it... here, perhaps... no, there... but I wonder... I must have made a mistake... It doesn't quite seem to match the others, the words that live elsewhere... I went somewhere far away from home to fetch them, and I brought them back here, but I don't know what is good for them, I don't know their habits...

The home words, solid words that I know very well, that I have placed, here and there, among these strangers, look awkward, self-conscious, a bit ridiculous... they are like people transported into an unknown land, into a society whose customs they haven't learnt, they don't know how to behave, they no longer quite know who they are...

And I am like them, I have lost my way, I'm wandering in places where I have never lived... I really don't know that pale young man with the blond curls, lying down beside a window through which he can see the mountains of the Caucasus... He coughs, and blood appears on the handkerchief he holds up to his lips... He won't be able to survive the first spring breezes... I have never for one moment been close to that Georgian princess wearing a red velvet toque with a long white floating veil... She is being carried off by a *dzhighite*, buttoned up tight in his black tunic... both sides of his chest are bulging with a cartridge pouch... I try to catch up with them when they dash off on a charger... a "mettlesome" charger... I throw this word at him... a word which I feel has a funny kind of look, rather disquieting, but never mind... they flee through the gorges, the defiles, borne by a mettlesome charger... they murmur vows of love... that is what they need... she clings to him... Beneath her white veil, her black hair flows down to her wasp waist...

I don't feel very much at ease with them, they intimidate me... but it doesn't matter, I must accommodate them as best I can, this is where they have to live... in a novel... in my novel, I, too, am writing one and I have to stay here with them... with the young man who is going to die in the spring, with the princess being carried off by the *dzhighite*... and also, with that old witch with the grey locks hanging down, with the clawlike fingers, sitting by the fire, who predicts for them... and also, with others who appear...

I make overtures to them... with my feeble, hesitant words I try hard to bring myself nearer to them, very near, to touch them, to feel them... But they are smooth and rigid, icy... it's as if they have been cut out of flashy metal... however hard I try there's nothing to be done, they always stay the same, their slippery surfaces glisten, scintillate... it's as if they are bewitched.

I, too, have been bewitched, I am imprisoned here with them, in this novel, there's no way I can get out...

And then those magic words... "Anyone who sets out to write a novel should first learn to spell"... break the charm and release me.

However much I huddle up, roll myself into a ball, hide my head under my blankets, fear, a fear such as I never remember having known since, creeps up on me, insinuates itself... That's where it comes from... I don't even need to look, I can sense it in everything there... it gives that light its greenish tinge... it is fear, that avenue of pointed, rigid, sombre trees with livid trunks, that procession of ghosts attired in long white robes advancing in a lugubrious file towards the grey flagstones... it flickers in the flames of the tall pallid candles they are carrying... it spreads all around, fills my room... I would like to escape, but I haven't the courage to cross the space impregnated with it that separates my bed from the door.

I finally manage to bring my head out for a moment to call out... Someone's coming. "*Now* what is it?" "They forgot to cover up the picture." "Yes, that's true... What a crazy child..." They get hold of something, no matter what, a towel, a garment, and hang it over the top of the frame... "There, now there's nothing to be seen... You aren't frightened any more?" "No, it's all over." I can stretch out full length in my bed, put my head on the pillow, relax... I can look at the wall to the left of the window... fear has disappeared.

A grown-up in a casual, offhand manner, with the impassive gaze of a conjuror, has whisked it away by sleight of hand.

H ow beautiful she is... I can't tear myself away from her, I hold Mama's hand more tightly, I keep her back so that we can stay there just a few more instants, so that I can go on looking in the window at that face... contemplating it...

—It's difficult to see in retrospect what was so fascinating about that doll.

—I can't really manage to understand. All I can see is her rather vague face, smooth and pink... luminous... as if lit from within... and also the proud curve of her nostrils, her lips, with their corners upturned... The thing I especially recall is my wonderment... everything about her was beautiful. Beauty—was that. That was what it was—to be beautiful.

I suddenly feel something like embarrassment, slight distress... it's as if somewhere inside me I have bumped into something, something has come and knocked into me... it takes shape, it acquires a form... a very precise form: "She is more beautiful than Mama."

—Where did that come from, all of a sudden?

—For a long time it was enough, when I happened to think back to that moment...

—You must admit that you didn't do it often...

—True. And I never dwelt on it for long... I vaguely imagined that the importance I had seemed to attach to the idea of "beauty" must have come to me from Mama. Who else could have inculcated it in me? She had such a power of suggestion over me... She must have led me... without ever demanding it... she had certainly incited me, without my knowing how, to consider her very beautiful, of incomparable beauty... That was where it had come from, my unease, my embarrassment...

But now, however hard I try, I can only manage to hear

Mama allude to "beauty" in connection with my aunt: "Anyiuta is a real beauty," or again, when referring to one of her friends... everything about whom, her face, her name, has been completely erased from my memory... "She is very beautiful," but always in the tone of a simple observation. With indifference. With perfect detachment.

I can't remember her looking at herself in a mirror, powdering her face... only her rapid glance when she passed a looking glass and her hasty gesture to push a stray wisp of hair back into her bun, push in a protruding hairpin.

She hardly seemed to bother about her appearance... It was as if she were on the outside... Outside all that.

—Yes. Or beyond it...

—That's the word: beyond it. Far removed from all possible comparison. It seemed as if no criticism, no praise, could alight on her. That was how she appeared to me.

I thought she was often delightful to look at, and it seemed to me that that was how she was for many others as well, I sometimes saw her in the eyes of passers-by, of tradesmen, of friends and, of course, of Kolya. I loved her fine, delicate features, as if they were blended... I can't find any other word... with her golden, rosy skin, soft and silky to the touch, more silky than silk, warmer and more tender than the feathers of a baby bird, than its down... The curves formed by her slightly bulging eyelids and her rather high cheekbones had the purity, the air of innocence that they sometimes have in children. Her eyes, of the same bronze colour as her smooth, silky hair, were not large, and they were just a little uneven... when something surprised her, one of her eyebrows, I think it was her left eyebrow, was raised higher than the other, it looked like a circumflex accent. Her gaze was rather strange... hard and inscrutable sometimes, and sometimes lively and naive... often as if absent...

—Perhaps that was her bad eyesight...

—Oh, no, she really did have that kind of absence which occasionally made her inaccessible to everyone... even to Kolya... and it got on his nerves... "What are you thinking about? You aren't listening..."

At all events, I now see clearly that I had never asked myself whether Mama was beautiful. And I still don't know what incited me, that day, to seize on the description "She's beautiful" which suited the hairdresser's doll so perfectly, which seemed to have been made for her, and to transport it, to try to make it also stay on Mama's face. And anyway, I no longer have the slightest recollection of that operation, although I must have performed it... the only thing that remains is the disquiet, the slight distress that accompanied it, and its final phase, its outcome, when I saw... how could I not see it?... it's obvious, it's certain, it *is* so: She is more beautiful than Mama.

Now that it is in me, there's no question of my hiding it from her, I can't distance myself from her to that extent, close myself up, enclose myself on my own with that, I can't be the only one to bear it, it belongs to her, to both of us... if I bottle it up in myself it will grow bigger, heavier, it will press harder and harder, I absolutely must let her see it, I'm going to show it to her... the way I show her a graze, a splinter, a bump... Look, Mama, look what I've got here, look what I've done to myself... "I think she's more beautiful than you"... and she will bend down, blow on it, pat it, come on now, it's nothing at all, just as she delicately extracts a thorn, just as she takes a coin out of her bag and presses it on the bump to stop it getting any bigger... "But of course, you big silly, of course, she's more beautiful than I am"... and it will stop hurting, it will disappear, we shall go on our way quietly, hand-in-hand...

But Mama lets go of my hand, or she holds it less tightly, she looks at me with her displeased expression and says: "A child who loves its mother thinks that no one is more beautiful than she."

I don't remember how we got home... perhaps we remained silent, or perhaps we even went on talking as if nothing had happened. I carried within me what she had deposited there... a well-wrapped parcel... It's only when we are home, when I am alone, that I will open it to see what it contains...

—It's that habit of never opening such parcels at once, but waiting to examine at your leisure what they contain, that probably explains your lack of repartee, your "after wit."

—Certainly. But in this case no repartee, even if I had had the gift, would have been possible...

—She probably expressed herself badly. What she

meant, no doubt, was: "A child who loves its mother never compares her with anyone else."

—That's right: a child who loves its mother doesn't observe her, doesn't dream of judging her...

—And also, what must have irritated her was that you had removed her from where she was... outside, beyond, and that you had pushed her among the others, where people compare, situate, assign places... she didn't measure herself against anyone, she didn't want to have a place anywhere.

—But that was something I wasn't capable of discerning, the words she used masked it. She had said: "A child who loves its mother thinks that no one is more beautiful than she." And it was these words that stood out, it was they that preoccupied me... A child. A. A. Yes, a child among all the others, a child like all the other children. A real child who possesses the feelings that all real children have, a child who loves its mother... What child doesn't love her? Where has that ever been known? Nowhere. It wouldn't be a child, it would be a monster. Or else, she wouldn't be a real mother, she would be a stepmother. Hence, a child who is like children are, like they should be, loves its Mama. And then, it thinks her more beautiful than anyone else in the world. It is this love it has for her that makes it think her so beautiful... the most beautiful... And I, it's obvious, I don't love her, since I think the hairdresser's doll more beautiful.

But how is it possible? But is it certain? But perhaps, after all, I don't really think that... Is it *quite* certain that she is more beautiful? Is she really? I must reexamine her... I reconjure up her pink, luminous face... I summon up each of her features... there's nothing to be done, I can't help it, there is nothing in her that isn't beautiful, that's what it is to be beautiful... and Mama... I can see her delicate face, her silky, golden skin... what her gaze radiates... but there it is, it's impossible not to see it, her ears aren't small enough, their lobes are too long, the line of her lips is too straight, her eyes aren't large, her lashes are rather short, her hair is straight... "beautiful" doesn't apply to Mama everywhere, not properly, it comes unstuck here and then there, however hard I try there is nothing to be done, I can't help seeing it: Mama isn't as beautiful.

Now that this idea has entrenched itself in me, it is not just a matter of willpower for me to dislodge it. I can force myself to uproot it, to put another idea in its place, but only for a time... it's still there, crouching in a corner, ready to get up at any moment, to push everything else out of its way, to occupy the whole space... It seems that trying to keep it down, to suppress it, only increases its growth. It is the proof, the sign of what I am: a child who doesn't love its mother. A child who bears the stigma of something that separates it, that outlaws it from other children... the light-hearted, carefree children I see laughing, shouting, chasing one another, swinging in the garden, in the square... and I am on my own. Alone with that something, which no one knows about and which no one, if told about it, would be able to believe.

I give up trying to struggle, trying to conjure up once again the face in the window and to place it side by side with

Mama's face... for that, I know, will only entrench the idea more firmly...

And in any case, the doll has vanished of her own accord, carrying with her the idea I had fixed on her... But its place has immediately been taken... another, similar idea has come to replace it. Perhaps it is even this new idea that has dislodged it...

Something that used to be in me has gone, something that is in all the other children, the real children... those rapid, limpid, running waters, like mountain streams, torrents, they have turned into the stagnant, muddy, polluted waters of ponds... the waters that attract mosquitoes. You don't need to tell me again that I wasn't capable of conjuring up these images... what is certain is that they convey the exact sensation produced in me by my pitiable state.

Ideas arrive at any moment, they sting, ah, here's one... and the tiny barb digs in, it hurts... "Mama's skin is like a monkey's."

That's how they are now, these ideas, they take all sorts of liberties. I look at Mama's *décolletage*, her golden, suntanned arms, and all of a sudden a little devil in me, a malicious little sprite, like the *"domovoï"* that play all sorts of tricks in houses, splashes that idea up at me: "Mama's skin is like a monkey's." I try to wipe it off, to rub it out... it isn't true, I don't believe it... *I* didn't think that. But there is nothing to be done, the furry coat of a monkey glimpsed in a cage in the zoo came, I don't know how, and alighted on Mama's neck, on her arms, and here is the idea... it hurts me...

I call Mama to the rescue, she must make it better... "You know, Mama, I have another idea now..." She immediately looks annoyed... *"Now* what is it?" "Well, I think... that your... skin is like a monkey's..." she will look to see what I have there, what has grown in me, against my will, we'll look at it together... it's so ridiculous, grotesque... we can only scoff at it, she will go off into one of her gales of laughter, which always make me laugh with her, we shall both laugh at it, and the idea will go back where it came from... where it was born... somewhere outside me, in a place I don't know... Or else, Mama will say: "Well, I'm delighted. You remember how sweet those little monkeys were."

—A reply that you are imagining now...

—Of course... but, without being able to imagine it exactly, I *was* expecting something of that order... which would immediately set my mind at rest. But Mama laughs scornfully and says: "Well, thank you very much... How kind of you..."

I don't believe I had ever been more alone before that— nor after, even. No help to be expected from anyone... Delivered up, defenceless, to "ideas." A fertile ground on which they could do whatever they liked, they disported themselves, called to each other, and still others came up... they all provided indubitable proof that I wasn't a child who loves its mother. Not like a child should be.

The disease was in me. This disease had chosen me because it found in me the nourishment it needed. It would never have been able to live in the healthy, pure, childish mind which other children possess.

When I sit sullenly in a corner and Mama asks me... but perhaps I am acting so ostensibly just to attract her attention, hoping she will ask me... "*Now* what's the matter with you? Why aren't you playing? Why aren't you reading?..."

then I will simply reply... but, even so, it's a relief: "I've got my ideas."

As people say: "I've got my pains. I've got my migraine," but with this difference: that mine is a shameful disease, a secret disease, that only she knows about. I can't possibly confide it to anyone else.

I no longer remember all the crazy, ridiculous ideas that came and inhabited me... only the last one... Fortunately, it arrived just before my departure, my separation from my mother, which put an abrupt end to what, if it had developed, ran the risk of becoming real madness...

This last idea was far and away the most cruel of all... It must have insinuated itself into me one evening when I was in the kitchen, probably playing the writers' quartet with the maids. I heard Gasha saying to the two others in veiled terms: "She"... and I knew that this "she" referred to Mama... "she's very nice on the whole, she never shouts at you, she's polite, and as for the food, there's nothing to complain about, except for the meat... Have you noticed those portions?..." and then it was over, it just passed through me rapidly without leaving any apparent trace... But then, when we were at table, at the moment when Gasha was holding out her plate to Mama as usual for the pieces of meat destined for "the kitchen," I saw... I didn't dare look at Gasha, I was afraid of surprising the way she looked at the plate on which Mama was putting... yes, there was no doubt about it... the pieces were smaller than the others, there was more fat on them... And immediately "the idea" was there: Mama doesn't treat Gasha well... even though she's so pale... nor the other maid...

This time the idea is no longer one of those that I can possibly reveal, even to Mama. I can no longer, if she asks me, reply: I've got my ideas... in the hope that she will be in a good mood and say: Come on, what is it? and that I will be able to show her... She would ask in amazement: Who gave you that idea? She would suspect, even if I concealed it... and with Mama I can't... she would know that it was Gasha...

So, as always, I am not strong enough to recognize and accept the truth. The meals in which there is meat cut into slices which Mama distributes to the maids become torture. "Mama is miserly." "Mama isn't grateful." "Mama is mean"... the ready-made idea is there, it's lying in wait... and I try to hold it back... just one more instant... we shall have to see... ah, what bliss... Mama is so engrossed in the conversation that she has picked up two pieces which are exactly the same as the others still on the dish, I dare to look at Gasha's plate, I rejoice... the vanquished idea retreats... I can feel calm, refreshing waves of confidence flowing through me... the other times, too, Mama wasn't thinking what she was doing, she is so often absent-minded... meanness, no, that isn't her at all, Gasha doesn't know her...

But then, at another meal, the idea comes back, it prowls around, it lies in wait... I'm frightened... I try to stop it from entering, I look away, but something compels me, I have to see... It's towards the end of the roast, towards that smaller bit and that other one next to it, it's towards them that Mama extends the fork, they are the ones she prongs, picks up and deposits on the plate Gasha is holding out to her... I don't look at Gasha's face... even if there isn't the slightest shadow of a smile on it, I know what she's thinking... I think it, as well. But for my part, the idea destroys me, devours me... when it lets go of me, it's only for a time, it will come back, it's always there, lying in wait, ready to pounce during any other meal.

I am sitting on the edge of my bed with my back to the window, and, standing on my knees, where I am holding him, is my companion, my confidant, my teddy bear with the golden fur, all soft and cuddly, and I am passing on to him what Mama has just told me... "You know, we're going back to Paris soon, to Papa... sooner than usual... and there, just imagine, there's going to be another mama..."

Then Mama, who is there, and who can hear me, says angrily: "What are you talking about? What other mama? no one can have another. You only have one mama in the whole world." I don't know whether she actually said these words or only the last of them, but I can remember the unusual emphasis with which she spoke to me, which left me speechless, as if petrified.

I don't remember any preparations for my departure... I know that Mama and Kolya were going away too, as soon as Mama had got back. Kolya had written a big book on the history of Austria-Hungary, and he had been invited to go and work for a few months in Budapest... a name I often heard at that time.

The news of my departure hadn't made me sad. I was used to these comings and goings, and I was pleased, as I always was, to be going to see Papa again, and the Luxembourg gardens... and the nice lady who had danced with me, who had been sitting on the bench with me at that moment... when the thing had happened... when it filled me, radiating from all around, from the light, the little brick walls, the espaliers, the chestnut trees in blossom... it still came back to me sometimes.

I have forgotten my probably heartrending farewells with Gasha... but, curiously enough, what has remained is the last moment, when I went back to kiss Kolya, who was very busy writing, surrounded by papers... when I sniffed at him like a little dog, the better to remember him... to preserve his smell of tobacco and toilet water, and when I once again looked at the shape of his nails, of his fingers... it seemed to me that they, especially, were the source of what emanated from him, what filled him, even enlarged him a little: his kindness, his good nature.

It is easy to imagine the white plains—it was February—through which we travelled, the wooden *izbas*, the white trunks of the birch trees, the snow-covered fir trees... I certainly saw them... but they are merged with so many similar images. What is not merged with anything else is Mama sitting opposite me by the window, her gesture when she holds out her arm, wipes my face, tears streaming down it, with her handkerchief, which is already soaking wet, and repeats: "You mustn't, my darling, you mustn't, my little child, my little kitten... you mustn't..."

Now and then my distress abates, I fall asleep. Or else, I amuse myself by chanting the same two words in time with the sound of the wheels... always the same two words which came, no doubt, from the sunlit plains I could see out of the window... the French word *soleil* and the same word in Russian, *solntze*, in which the "l" is hardly pronounced, sometimes I say sol-ntze, pulling back and pushing out my lips, with the tip of my curled up tongue pressing against my front teeth, and sometimes, so-leil, stretching my lips, my tongue barely touching my teeth. And then again, solntze. And then again, so-leil. A mind-destroying game which I can't stop. It stops of its own accord, and the tears flow.

—It's strange that it should have been on this particular occasion that you first felt such distress at leaving... It's almost as if you had a presentiment....

—Or else, Mama...

—Yes, something that would have made you feel that this time it wasn't a departure like the others...

—I find it hard, hurtful even, to believe that she could already then have envisaged... No, it isn't possible that she could deliberately have wanted to abandon me to my father.

—Isn't it enough for us to note that this was February, and that you knew the separation would be longer than usual, since this time you were going to have to stay with your father for more than two months... until the end of the summer.

I have a perfect recollection of a little station surrounded by scintillating snow, where we waited in a room lit by big bay windows, the uniforms of the employees were different, I knew we were at the frontier.

And then, Berlin. A huge, rather dark room, on one side of which were two beds covered with enormous red eiderdowns, and on the other side, some armchairs and a round table... Mama is sitting at this table with an "uncle" whom I don't know... Mama has told me that he is a friend of hers from the old days, when she was a student in Geneva, and that he is also a great friend of my father. From now on he is going to be in charge of me and take me to Paris. He has a fine, kindly face, very grey, full of little holes like people who have had smallpox... the tip of his nose is pointed, as if eaten away...

Mama is talking to him in a low voice, and I have discovered a very amusing game: already in my long nightdress, I jump with my feet together from one bed to the other, the beds are quite far apart, you have to take careful aim and then, ploof, fall on to the other side, sink into the enormous eiderdown, roll over, making a noise, giving little screams...

Mama says: "Stop it, you're disturbing us... we are going to be parted tomorrow, there's nothing to be so cheerful about." I calm down at once, I stretch out at full length on one of the beds. I hear Mama, sounding extremely surprised, say: "Really? She is..." I don't catch the word that follows...

When we are alone, I ask Mama: "What was it that Uncle said, when you looked so surprised?" "Oh, I can't remember." "Yes you can. Tell me. You said: 'She is...' Who was the she?" Mama hesitates and then says: "She—was Vera, your father's wife." "She is what?" "Nothing..." "Yes, you *must* tell me. What is she?" Mama seems to be thinking of something that amuses her... "Well if you really want to know, he told me that she is stupid."

The only thing I can remember of the next day is the dark grey platform, the atrocious whistles, Mama leaning out of the window of a train which is slowly moving away, and me running down the platform, shouting, sobbing, and the uncle running after me to catch me, taking my hand, bringing me back, I no longer know where, probably to another train leaving in the opposite direction. I have a feeling that I did nothing but cry until we arrived in Paris at the Gare du Nord, whose yellowish greyness, whose immense glass vault, for the very first time looked sinister.

I don't know whether anyone came to meet us, I only remember my father in the dreary flat in the rue Marguerin which seemed as if it wasn't completely inhabited... and his strange welcome, so different from all his previous welcomes... a little cold, stiff... and the young woman... "You recognize Vera? you remember her?" I say yes, but I have difficulty in recognizing her as that very young woman with the round, pink cheeks, so slender and agile in her man's suit, with a stray wisp of hair escaping from her bowler hat, who whirled round with me, lifted me up, collapsed with me out of breath, fanning herself with her handkerchief, going off into gales of laughter... she wasn't like this lady with her hair rolled back over her temples in smooth, disciplined loops, not a strand out of place, her long face is very pale, her lower teeth protrude and cover her top ones, her thin, straight lips stretch as if they are pretending to smile, and in her very light, very transparent eyes, there is something... there was nothing like that in Gasha's eyes, though they were even lighter and more transparent... yes, something I had never noticed in anyone else... something like an alarming little flame...

Here, as in St. Petersburg, my room looks out on to the street. Outside there is no longer a silvery light, nor, somewhere in the distance, vast expanses of ice, of scintillating snow... but a rather dirty light, shut in between rows of little houses with dismal façades...

—Dead, you should call them, without fear of exaggeration.

—Yes, lifeless. It's curious that these same houses, when I lived in the rue Flatters, had always seemed to me to be alive, I felt protected, gently enveloped in their yellowish greyness... and they led to the amusements, the insouciance of the Luxembourg gardens, where the air was luminous, vibrant.

Here, the stiff little roads led to the parc Montsouris. Its very name seemed ugly to me, its vast lawns encircled with little hoops were imbued with sadness, it was as if they had been stuck there to remind you of real meadows, and they made you feel so nostalgic for them that it was sometimes heartrending... you will grant that the word is not too strong.

That was where Vera took me and I pretended to play—with a ball, building sand castles, or running along the gravel on the paths bordered with hoops. Even the merry-go-rounds here didn't tempt me.

My evenings, when I was in bed, were devoted to Mama, to crying as I took her photo, in which she was sitting beside Kolya, from under my pillow, to kissing her and telling her that I could no longer bear being so far away from her, she must come and fetch me...

It had been agreed between Mama and me that if I was happy I would write: "I am <u>very</u> happy here," underlining the "very." And only "I'm happy," if I wasn't. And it was this that I one day decided to write at the end of a letter... I no longer felt strong enough to wait for several more months, until September, for her to come and take me back. So I wrote to her: "I'm happy here."

Some time later my father calls me. I saw very little of him. He left at about seven in the morning, when I was asleep, and came home in the evening very tired, preoccupied, the meal often passed in silence. Vera spoke very little. The words she uttered were always short, the vowels as if squashed between the consonants, as if to make each word take less room. Even my name she pronounced by almost eliminating the "a"s. So that it became a strange sound—or rather noise: N't'sh...

After dinner my father, I felt, was glad for me to go to

bed... and I myself preferred to go to my room.

—You didn't only cry there...

—No, I must have read, as always... I remember a book by Mayne Reid that my father had given me. He had liked it when he was small... personally, I didn't enjoy it very much... perhaps I was too young... eight and a half... I skipped the long descriptions of the prairies and escaped to the liberating dashes that introduced the dialogue.

Several days after I had sent that letter to Mama, then, my father keeps me back after dinner and takes me into his study, which is separated from the dining room by a glass door... He says: "You have written to your mother that you are unhappy here." I am stupefied: "How do you know?" "Well, I've had a letter from your mother. She reproaches me, she tells me that we aren't treating you well, that you're complaining..."

I am shattered, overwhelmed, by the shock of such treachery. So now I have no one in the world I can complain to. Mama isn't even dreaming of coming to rescue me, what she wants is for me to stay here and feel less unhappy. Never again shall I be able to confide in her. Never again shall I be able to confide in anyone. I must have displayed such total, such profound despair that, all of a sudden, my father, abandoning the reserve, the aloofness he always shows towards me here, clasps me in his arms more tightly than he had ever clasped me, even in the old days... he brings out his handkerchief and awkwardly, tenderly, almost trembling, he wipes away my tears, and I think I see tears in his own eyes. He simply says: "Go to bed, don't upset yourself"... an expression he has often used when talking to me... "nothing in life is worth it... you'll see, in life, sooner or later everything sorts itself out..."

At that moment, and forever after, despite all appearances, an invisible bond, which nothing was ever able to destroy, united us... I don't know exactly what my father felt, but I, at that age, I wasn't nine years old, I am sure that everything that was gradually revealed to me, during the ensuing years, I perceived at that moment, at a stroke, en bloc... all my relations with my father, with my mother, with Vera, their own relationships, were only the unravelling of what was then enravelled.

We are spending July in a guest house in Meudon so that my father, who is now trying to start a little factory in Vanves, where they will make the same chemicals as they did in his factory in Ivanovo, can be with us every evening. The house stands in a huge park, without lawns, strewn with pine needles and planted with big, dark trees... In the dining room, a man comes and sits at another table, he has a puffy, pallid face, which I was later reminded of by the actor who played the murderer in the German film M. Whenever I look at him, he stares at me as if to frighten me with his very glittering eyes. His immobile, inexpressive gaze makes me think of the gaze of wild animals.

Vera is getting thinner and thinner, her face is all yellow, her stomach is sticking out, I hear, I don't remember how, that she is expecting a child. And one morning, shortly after we had returned to Paris, my father, who hasn't gone to work, tells me that since the previous evening Vera has been in a clinic and that a little girl has been born, a little sister for me... I shall see her as soon as Vera is feeling better, she suffered a great deal and the baby is still very weak.

We walk down a dismal street, as long as its name, Ver-cin-gé-to-rix, and finally come to the clinic. Vera smiles sweetly at me, by her bed, in a cradle, I see a hideous little creature, red, violet, with an enormous, howling mouth, it seems it howls like that, day and night, until it nearly strangles itself. Vera looks worried, with her hand on the side of the cradle, she rocks it. They tell me to kiss the baby, but I'm afraid to touch it, finally, I reluctantly decide to place my lips on its furrowed brow which seems likely to be shattered by its strident cries... What is she going to be called? Hélène... This is in memory of the little girl who was born three years before me and who died of scarlet fever before I was born. I had seen her photo at Ivanovo. She was in the arms of her nurse, who was wearing a tall bonnet embroidered with beads... She looked like Mama, but her eyes were enormous, as if full of astonishment... I had been told that Papa had himself nursed her, cradled her in his arms and had been so grief-stricken at her death that he fell ill himself.

—It's true that he had suffered enormously from her death, but he fell ill because he had caught scarlet fever from her.

—I know it now, but that wasn't what they had told me, which was what I still believed...

few days before Vera came back with the baby, I am surprised to see that all my belongings are no longer in my room, a rather vast room looking on to the street. The tall, fat woman who does all the work in the flat tells me that from now on I am going to live in the little room that looks on to the courtyard, just by the kitchen... "Who is going to live in my room?" "Your little sister with her nurse..." "What nurse?" "She's coming quite soon..."

If someone had thought to explain to me that it wasn't possible to accommodate a baby and a grown-up in my new room, that there was no other solution, I think I would have understood. But to be removed like that, brutally, from what for me had gradually become "my room," and thrown into what seemed to me to be a sinister cubbyhole, not hitherto inhabited, gave me an easily imaginable feeling of favouritism, of unfair preference. It was at this point that the good woman who was just completing my removal stopped in front of me—I was sitting on my bed in my new room—looked at me with an air of great pity, and said: "What a tragedy, though, to have no mother."

"What a tragedy!"... the word strikes you, it strikes you like a whiplash. Straps wind themselves around me, crush me... So *that* is it, that terrible thing, the most terrible thing possible, whose external signs were faces bloated with tears, black veils, groans of despair... "Tragedy," which had never approached me, never touched me, has struck me. This woman sees it. I am enclosed in it. In tragedy. Like everyone who has no mother. I haven't got one, then. It's obvious, I have no mother. But how is that possible? How can that have happened—to *me*? Whatever it was that made my tears flow, the tears Mama wiped away with a calm gesture, saying: "You mustn't..." could she have said that if it had been a tragedy?

I take Mama's letters out of a painted wooden casket, they are strewn with affectionate words, she talks of "our love," "our separation" in them, it is obvious that we aren't separated for good, not forever... And is *that* what a tragedy is? My parents, who know better, would be amazed if they heard that word... Papa would be annoyed, angry... he hates these big words. And Mama would say: Yes, a tragedy when people love each other as we do... but not a real tragedy... our "unfortunate separation," as she calls it, won't last... A tragedy, all that? No, it's impossible. And yet this woman, who is so strong, so solid, sees it. She sees tragedy on me, as clearly as she sees "my two eyes on my face." No one else here knows it, they all have other things to do. But she, who observes me, she has recognized it, that's it all right: the tragedy that strikes children in books, in *No Relations*, in *David Copperfield*. This same tragedy has pounced on me, it grips me, it has me in its claws.

I remain motionless for some time, hunched up on the edge of my bed... And then, everything in me revolts, rises up, with all my strength I reject it, I smash it, I tear off this yoke, this carapace. I won't stay in this thing in which that woman has imprisoned me... she doesn't know anything, she can't understand.

—Was that the first time you had been trapped like that, in a word?

—I don't remember it happening to me before. But how many times since, have I not escaped, terrified, out of words which pounce on you and hold you captive.

—Even the word "happiness"—every time it came quite close, so close, ready to alight, you tried to ward it off... No, not that, not one of those words, they frighten me, I prefer to do without them, I don't want them anywhere near me, I don't want them to touch anything... nothing here, in me, is for them.

The little streets lined with dreary houses, rue du Loing, rue du Lunain, rue Marguerin...

—Charming names, though, when you listen to them now...

—When I make an effort to imagine the delicate, light sound they must have in the ears of a tourist... Or of one of those people who were lucky enough, as they told me later, to find in these little streets that unobtrusive, almost tender benevolence conferred on me by the rue Flatters or the rue Berthollet.

But when I think back on them as they were at the time, these names, Lunain, Loing, Marguerin, like those little streets, immediately reassume their narrow, mean aspect... It seems to me that, sheltering behind lifeless façades, behind dark windows, in the innermost recesses of dingy little cages, people who are barely alive are treading warily, barely moving...

I run past these houses, I enter a porchway just like all the others, I cross the dangerous place outside the lodge where the concierge, who is even dreaded by the grown-ups, raises a corner of her greyish curtain and observes me... I wipe my feet on the mat, I carefully open the double glass door, I climb, as fast as I can, up the polished stairs, until I get to the second... or is it the third landing? I ring, someone comes running, opens the door... "Come in, they're here."

In the children's room, all the objects, the broken toys, the dilapidated furniture, have an air of liberty, of insouciance, all they want is to enjoy themselves, the beds, the divans are just waiting for us to collapse on them in fits of laughter, with little screams... not too loud ones, though... "Make a little less noise, please, children..." A door half-opens, we get a glimpse of a completely white room, a dentist's chair... "Calm down a little, I have patients..." Madame Pereverzev, dressed in long white overalls, has a shiny metal instrument in her hand, her face is all round and all pink, and her nose is turned up so far that people say, and this amuses her, that through it you can read the thoughts in her head. Her daughter Tanya has exactly the same nostrils... it's as if it is her innocence, her mischievousness that enlarge them, dilate them like that, that turn up her lips... Of her brother, who is a year or two older than we are, all I remember is the name Boris and the gales of laughter he used to go off into, which we found contagious, which the ban on making a noise fostered and fortified, which were interrupted by silences that were bursting at the seams, which promised dangerous, voluptuous explosions.

Sometimes another door is opened and the slender, dark

silhouette of Monsieur Pereverzev appears... but now, for me, his face is merged with that of Chekhov, his pince-nez is a little crooked on his nose, its black cord hangs down his cheek, his face is thoughtful, a little sad, he says in a low, kindly voice... "Tt,tt, come on now, children, let me get on with my work."

To whom are they addressed, then, the postcards, the letters that Mama sends me? To whom does she think she is telling, as you tell a little child, that, in the place where she and Kolya are having a month's holiday, the little girls wear red ribbons and pretty wooden clogs, that the sea is all blue and that you can see sailing boats going by on it, like the ones in the lake in the Luxembourg gardens, but here, they are real ones, big boats...

She doesn't know who I am now, she has even forgotten who I was.

Sometimes, something like gaiety, like satisfaction, filters through these childish accounts.

I feel I don't ever want to get a letter again, I want to break these bonds forever, but every time, the tender, caressing words at the end hold me back, envelop me... I soften, I can't tear up the paper these words have been written on. Piously, I put it away in my casket.

I speak as little as possible about Mama... With my father, everything that might remind him of her runs the risk of raising and revealing... not in his words, but in his frown, in the way he puckers and pushes out his lips, in the narrow slits between his contracting eyelids... something that I don't want to see...

—Resentment, reproach... and, let us dare say... contempt.

—But that isn't what I call it. I don't give it any name, I vaguely feel that it is there, in him, buried, compressed... whatever happens I don't want it to be stirred up, to come to the surface...

My father himself, when it is really necessary, designates my mother by the name of the place she lives in: "Have you written to Petersburg?" "There's a letter for you from Petersburg." The words "your mother," which he formerly used, now, I don't know why, can no longer cross his lips.

And then, one day, under my father's gaze which I feel on my face, a lingering gaze that doesn't leave it, I raise one of my eyebrows like Mama does, I open my eyes wide, I stare ahead of me into the far, far distance, my eyes, like Mama's, fill with astonishment, helplessness, candour, innocence...

My father is still looking at what I am displaying, motionless, before his eyes...

But it isn't I , it's he, it is his own gaze that has made that appear on my face, it is he who keeps it there...

—It would be easy to imagine that what his gaze conjured up would more likely be the hard, inscrutable expression your mother sometimes had, the one she must most often have shown to him and which he must have known best.

—If I had felt this, then that is the expression I would have adopted, and I would have made it even harder... out of defiance... as one sometimes does in such cases...

—Yes, and also out of despair...

—But it wasn't that expression my father was looking for on my face, that wasn't what he wanted to see, and what happened later proves that my feeling was correct. He turned to the friend who was there, it was the mutual friend of my parents who had brought me from Berlin... the three of us were alone... and my father, finally tearing his eyes away from me, turned to him and said: "It's astonishing how like her mother Natasha can sometimes look..." and something had crept into these words, something infinitely fragile, which I hardly dared to perceive, I was afraid of making it disappear... it brushed against me, caressed me and then vanished.

"It isn't your home"... It's hard to believe, but this is, nevertheless, what Vera said to me one day. When I asked her if we were going home soon, she said: "It isn't your home."

—Exactly what the cruel stepmother might have replied to poor Cinderella. That was what made you hesitate...

—Yes indeed: I was afraid that in reliving all this, I might find myself making Vera and me into characters in a fairy tale...

—It's true that Vera, at times, when you make the effort to call her to mind, gives you a feeling of losing touch with reality, of taking off into fiction...

—But might we not, this time, to keep within the bounds of reality, try to imagine that she used those words because it was still understood that my mother was going to take me back, I mustn't get too used to feeling at home in a house that I would soon have to leave... she wanted to spare me a new heartache...

—Let us suppose that that was so... And let us also suppose that she may have been beginning to fear that you would stay here... it was a heavy responsibility for that young woman... it was quite unforeseen... nothing had led her to think that she would have to assume it forever... and when she realized that you thought it was your home you were going back to, she couldn't help herself, she couldn't restrain the impulse that drove her to uproot you from that house, to prevent your "feeling at home" there... Oh no, not that... "It isn't your home."

—To rediscover what can have sparked off these words of hers, I would at least have to hear their intonation again... to feel the effect on me of the fluids they give off... But nothing of all that has remained. It is probable that by their very force they have crushed everything... even at that moment, there was nothing in them, nothing around them that was invisible, nothing to be discovered, to be examined... the way I received them, they were closed on all sides, completely clear and naked.

They sank into me like a dead weight, and they made it impossible, once and for all, for the word "home" to take shape in me, to come to my lips... Never again "home," for as long as I lived there, even when it was certain that outside that house there could never be any other home for me.

It's October, school has started, all the children I know are going to school... I would so like to go too, I am already nine... my father tells me that he has written to St. Petersburg to ask if they were still thinking of having me back, but so far there has been no reply... and yet school started in Russia at the beginning of September... Wouldn't it be better for me to have some sort of lessons in the meantime? Quite close to us there is a private school, run by the Brébant sisters, which could prepare me for entrance into the local primary school in the class appropriate to my age.

All I can remember of my fairly brief sojourn with the Brébant sisters is my handwriting, which had previously been perfectly legible and had suddenly become unrecognizable... I didn't understand what was happening to it... the letters were deformed, misshapen, the lines went off in all directions, I was no longer in control of my hand...

At the Brébant school, they are very patient with me, very concerned. When they manage to decipher my scrawl, they notice that I make fewer spelling mistakes than the others, I must have done a lot of reading for my age. But I must start to learn to write all over again. As I did previously, when I went to the school in the rue des Feuillantines, using black ink, I cover the very pale, bluey-grey pot-hooks, all lined up at the same angle... I take home copy books full of pot-hooks and also of letters, which I have to copy in the same way... gradually, with a lot of application, my handwriting becomes subdued, calms down...

It's soothing, it's reassuring to be here all by myself, shut in my room... no one will come and disturb me, I'm doing "my homework," I am doing "work" that everyone respects... Lili is crying, Vera is furious, I don't know why or with whom, people are coming and going on the other side of my door, none of all that concerns me... I wipe my pen on a little felt square, I dip it into the pot of black ink, I cover, taking great care... there mustn't be the slightest smudge... those pale, ghostly pot-hooks, I make them as visible, as clear as possible... I coerce my hand, and it obeys me better and better...

I don't ever think of it any more, I can say that it has completely "gone out of my head." And then, one fine day it comes back to me... It's barely believable... How is it possible that I could have experienced that such a short time ago, barely a year ago, when they used to arrive, to insinuate themselves into me, to swamp me... "my ideas," which I was the only one to have, which sent everything reeling, sometimes I felt I would go under... a poor, crazy child, a demented baby, crying out for help... "You know, Mama, I've got my ideas... I think that your skin is like a monkey's..." I imitate as best I can the tone of voice I had then, a tearful, pathetic, grotesque tone... I try to bring back, it's just to amuse myself, just for fun... I can allow myself to do so without danger... that apprehension when I felt them creeping up on me... they cropped up no matter when, they came from no matter where, they established themselves, they grew, they felt at home in me... in a propitious place made just for them, an unclean, unhealthy place... How delightful it is, the contrast with what I am now... how clear my mind seems now, how clean, flexible, healthy... Ideas... not "my" ideas... no more of those dubious "my"s, of those disturbing "my"s... ideas, like everyone else has, occur to me as they do to everyone else. I can think of anything whatsoever without being afraid. Is there anything that can make me feel ashamed, that can make a poor, abnormal being of me, a pariah? Nothing. Absolutely nothing. However hard I search... and I do search... let it come, then, if it wants to, that "idea..." but nothing comes... there aren't any... Ah, here comes one that is like "my ideas" of the old days, like those I used to mull over so sadly in a corner... I call it over, here it is: "Papa is a bad-tempered man. Papa gets angry for no reason. Papa is often in a vile mood." Well?... Well what? I have thought it, and it belongs to no one but me. I don't have to answer for it to anybody. But perhaps I'm exaggerating, and Papa... Perhaps... It was just a passing idea, it's gone... ideas have now become discreet, they merely pass through me, they obey me, *I* am the one who decides to hold them back, to make them stay as long as is necessary, when I happen to feel like examining them before I dismiss them. None of them can make me feel ashamed, none of them can affect *me*. Oh, how good I feel. That will never happen to me again. Never...

—But what if you had gone back there? Are you sure that you didn't dread, even for a single moment, even very fleetingly, that there, with your mother, it might come over you again?

—I don't think so. It seems to me that at that moment I believed that I possessed forever a strength that nothing could subdue—complete and utter independence.

When Monsieur Laran comes to see my father he brings his son Pierre, who is my age. My father has a very high opinion of Monsieur Laran, he's a scientist, he teaches in one of the "grandes écoles," I believe it's the École des Mines. My father says that Pierre is very intelligent, very good at science, always top of his class. I have to spend a good part of the afternoon with him and we have to get some fresh air, we have to go and play in the parc Montsouris.

We walk side by side down the long, dismal avenue. Pierre looks very like his father, but he seems older than him. I do realize that he must have been dressed like little boys of his age were, but when I visualize him now, I have to remove the bowler hat that I see on his head and replace it with a sailor's beret, I have to take off his father's high, white collar, bare his neck, put the wide collar of a sailor suit on his shoulders, transform his trousers into shorts... but none of these changes enables me to transform him into a little boy. It's an old gentleman I am walking with. Old and sad. You can see that he knows a great deal... about what? I have no idea, about all sorts of things that I know nothing about... He listens to my childish prattle... but it is rare for me to manage, as I can with almost all the grown-ups, to make him smile.

In the end, I give up trying. We remain silent. I think about all sorts of things that amuse me... And he? I don't ask myself what he is thinking about, I'm too busy preparing my act... for tomorrow... no, tomorrow will be Monday, but for Thursday, when I'm going to Misha's... "Well, did you enjoy yourself?" "No, idiot, and I shan't forgive you... You really might have come. Your father came..." Monsieur Agafonov is a scientist, too. In Russia he used to teach geology at the university, he has written books. When he arrived and we asked him why he hadn't brought Misha, he pulled a face, raised one hand in a rueful gesture, the whole of his being lit up with tenderness and pride, and he said... "How do you expect me to manage to get hold of my good-for-nothing, I don't know where he has disappeared to."

I know, though... "I've never known such an egotist as you. You might have done it for me." But I am already savouring what is about to follow... and Misha gives me my cue... "Come on, then, tell all, was it interesting? Where did you go?" "You don't deserve to be told..." "Oh, come on, you can't keep it to yourself. It must have been hilarious..." "In that case, I shall begin at the beginning... We go downstairs... Pierre stands aside and lets me go through the door first..." "I don't believe it..."

Misha's mother has come in, she sits down in an armchair, she gives me a kindly look with her greenish eyes, her soft, delicate face is very pale, almost grey, she always toys with a little batiste handkerchief... she is very ill... perhaps she knows it, Misha never talks to me about it... but even so, it doesn't take much to make her laugh... She says:

"There's nothing to laugh at. Pierre has very good manners..." That's all we need... "Very good manners. He has very good manners!" I can go on with my act. There is nothing I like so much as imitating people. And who better could I ever find to imitate than Pierre? I imitate him as he opens the door for me. I imitate myself bowing with dignity like a lady. And then, I start walking placidly, I pretend to stop at the edge of a pavement, as we have been taught to... I prudently look one way and then the other... We hoot with laughter... Madame Agafonov says: "Ah, you see, Misha, *you* will get run over, one day..." I say sententiously: "Yes, Misha, that is what is in store for you. And also, one day you'll be guillotined... When I told Pierre about everything you get up to..." "You didn't do that?" "Yes, I did, I told him everything..." I can talk about it in front of his mother... nothing moves her so much... Misha stole a bunch of flowers from a florist's window to give her for her birthday, and afterwards, when he had confessed, when he had taken it back, the florist gave it to him for nothing, and he came back again with the flowers... "I told him that you had stolen..." "What did he say?" "He opened his eyes wide, he said it's horrible..." I walk like Pierre, as if I were holding a stick in my hand... Then I imitate myself gambolling around him like a little dog, sitting up and begging, aspiring to be granted one little smile... pretending to be a beggar woman: Kind Sir, just one smile... But he doesn't want to... I invent other things, goodness knows what, we cry with laughter, Madame Agafonov wipes her eyes with her little handkerchief... "That's enough now, children, go for a walk..." "But not to the parc Montsouris, Mama..." Misha goes up to his mother, he is my age but he is very strong, and she is so frail... she stretches out her hands in front of her with a terrrified air... "No, no, don't touch me, you'll crush me," she laughs tenderly, he hugs her gently and we go off.

Monsieur Agafonov, a superb, kindly giant, passes us in the hall... "Where are you going to kick your heels?" He takes Misha by the ears and pretends to pick him up... "Ah, you little rascal..." To me, he says: "Be careful. God knows what crazy idea may go through this cretin's head..." But he knows, and I know too, that nothing can happen to me so long as I am with Misha.

We go to our hunting ground: the avenue d'Orléans, and we start our competition. The winner is the one who collects the most leaflets from the cheap-jacks handing them out. We hunt on opposite pavements. Then we change pavements. We aren't allowed to ask for the same one from the same cheap-jack or to pick up any from the ground. Then we go back to Misha's place, go to his room and count our booty: piles of leaflets, white, yellow, blue, pink...

—What did the winner get?

—I don't remember. Nothing, I think, other than the satisfaction of victory.

Lili is sitting on a chair piled high with cushions at the dining room table, which is covered with white oilcloth during her meals. She stretches out her thin little arm towards the bell rope hanging down from the light pendant, her eyes are staring, she yells in a strident voice: "It swinging! it swinging!" Vera, sitting by her side, grabs the rope in order to immobilize it... although it is already completely immobile... but this doesn't calm Lili, she goes on yelling: "It swinging!" Then Vera winds the rope round the lamp... and she spoons up a little of the food from the plate and holds it up to Lili's mouth... "Eat it up, my little rabbit..." that's what she calls her, or else: "My little white rabbit"... "you must eat it, it's good for you..." What she is trying to make her eat is brains... Lili is the only one who is entitled to them, she is so fragile, she needs this fortifying, delicate dish... But one day the kindly fat maid let me taste a little bit in the kitchen...

Sometimes she tries like that to make up as best she can for the injustices that revolt her... "Everything is only for the little girl in this house... It's like with the bananas, believe it or not, they're hidden at the top of the linen cupboard, behind the pile of sheets, so that the big one doesn't take any... It's a crying shame to see that..." I can't remember whom she was talking to, but I do remember that that was how I discovered something amazing that I hadn't even suspected: the existence of that hiding place.

I am lucky enough not to like those grey, milky, flabby brains... and as for bananas, if I want some, I can buy them with my pocket money... I don't even need to ask Papa for it, he always gives it to me first... but I don't think I ever bought myself any bananas, I rather think the idea didn't occur to me...

At first, Vera offers the beneficial brains to Lili with a calm, patient air, but you feel she's beginning to lose her temper... as she herself sometimes says: "Everything in me is trembling." Lili is still staring with dilated eyes at the bell rope wound round the light pendant, and her mother reassures her in a voice that is becoming more and more of a hiss... "You can see very well it isn't swinging any more, so eat it up..." Lili opens her mouth, yells No! and immediately shuts it again. Vera insists...

Her very pale blue eyes seem to become transparent, and a little flame in them lights up... in her fixed gaze, there is something obstinate, implacable, that makes you think of the gaze of a tiger.

—Someone did say, do you remember, that she sometimes had the eyes of a wildcat...

—And in what a tone of voice!... as if that was one of her most charming qualities. But for my part, in those days, I

126

had never seen any wildcats, I had only observed the eyes of panthers or tigers at the zoo. They were what Vera reminded me of. When her fury increased she could no longer speak, she blew, with a threatening air, through her clenched teeth, her bosom heaved... Lili was the only one who had the power to transform her like that, to get her into such a state of nerves... And Lili wasn't afraid of her. It was as if she saw it as one more proof of her mother's passionate love.

—A unique passion. Lili was her malady. And that fury—you felt that it wasn't really directed against Lili but against something that was beyond her... *that* was the target of Vera's fixed, obstinate, implacable gaze... a fate which she wanted to vanquish at all costs... she would compensate, she would more than compensate for everything it might refuse her child, she would transform it, whatever the cost, and convert it into the best, the most enviable fate in the world.

—As for me, I wasn't afraid of Vera, either. I knew that the only way I could provoke her to irritation, to impatience, in which there was hostility, but cold, distant hostility, was if she was afraid that I might in any way harm Lili. And I always kept as far away from Lili as possible... this was no trouble, I hadn't the slightest desire to approach that howling child with the contorted face...

—Which could be dangerous... it *had* happened that when you were alone together she started screaming to make them think you had hurt her...

—But even in that case, Vera didn't get very angry with me...

—She wouldn't allow herself to. Perhaps she was afraid of playing the unenviable role of the cruel stepmother.

—Perhaps... and then, she felt that I was surrounded by the presence, which though distant was protective, of my father... It seems to me that in her rather primitive way, without really realizing it, she was afraid of him...

—Yes, obscurely... she saw him as her master... And couldn't it also be thought that she had perhaps suspected that Lili had been putting on one of her acts...

—No, not quite that... I don't think she was capable of being quite so lucid... not in that case... Nor do I think she was capable of feeling that there could be any injustice where Lili was concerned. She must have confined herself to saying: "Don't touch her, please. Leave her alone." And I must have replied: "But I do leave her alone."

Ever since Lili's birth, Vera has been very thin, very pale, Papa took her to consult a professor of medicine who said that she was threatened with phthisis, that she must eat a lot... And since then, at teatime, they bring two plates into the dining room, one for her, one for me... I have no need of this extra meal, but Vera has suggested that I have it with her... Our plates are filled with golden macaroni, shining with fresh butter, with each mouthful a long ribbon of melted cheese hangs down from our forks, and we cut it off with our teeth. I devour everything on my plate and often, when I have emptied it, Vera offers me what remains on hers... "Finish it if you like, I simply can't eat any more, however much I force myself..."

When Vera isn't preoccupied by Lili, when she forgets her, she sometimes becomes quite young again...

In a forest on the outskirts of Paris, on a road lined on both sides by tall trees with their yellowing leaves... the sun is gentle, you can smell the lovely, invigorating scent of the moss... I am perched on my bike, helped by Vera, she runs after me a little way, her hand on my saddle, then she lets go of me... but when I get to the bend, that's it, once again I fall off... we laugh... "But it's not possible, you're doing it on purpose... It's because you're nervous, you get tense. Watch me." I give her a little help as she hoists herself into the saddle, and she pedals away like mad, she disappears round the bend... My father and I clap when she comes back smiling... And she, too, claps her hands and calls out, bravo! when I have finally managed to negotiate the bend...

And we teach my father to ride... But he is so stiff, so awkward, so unsure of himself... we run along with him, holding him on either side, but the moment we let go of him he stops, puts a foot on the ground... "No, decidedly..." he looks sheepish, embarrassed, he hasn't got the gift, how old

130

he seems... and all of a sudden, how sorry for him I feel...

—He was only forty-two or -three, though...

—But in those days, people were old sooner than now. And he wasn't at all athletic... he suddenly seemed very old to me, and I thought that that was how Vera, too, saw him, and that he himself had felt he was an old man in comparison with her, when she ran with me, holding his saddle, when we were both urging him on, when we were gently laughing at him... Who wouldn't have thought that Vera was my big sister, that we were his two daughters...

We are sitting, Vera and I, side by side at the dining room table which is covered with a thick, golden, plush cloth. I watch her delicate little hands and her agile fingers plunging into a wide jar that contains tobacco... it's a mixture Papa has himself prepared, and in which a few pieces of raw carrot have been scattered to keep it from drying up... Vera brings out a pinch of tobacco between three fingers, she rubs it lightly to separate the leaves properly, and then she spreads it over a little, open metal tube... she packs the tobacco tightly into both halves of the tube and shuts one on to the other with a little click... Then, from a big box of empty cigarettes that Papa has had sent to him from Russia—he can't smoke any others—she takes a cigarette whose cardboard end is as long as the paper one. It is into this cylinder of very thin paper that Vera carefully introduces the metal tube... delicately pushes the tobacco up, fills it...

—But how?

—I can't see it very well now. I rather think she does it by pushing a little ball along a groove in the tube... And then, she withdraws the tube without tearing the paper, she taps the full end of the cigarette to even out the tobacco, she removes one little leaf that is sticking out...

I observe each of her movements... I would love to try... and she lets me take a pinch of tobacco, like her, rub it, spread it out on both sides of the open metal tube, shut it... and then take an empty cigarette out of the box... introduce the end of the tube, push... Careful, not too hard... I do it as gently as I can, but the paper is so fragile, and there, it has torn...

I'd like to try again, let me just once more... All right, but after that, no more. And once again the paper tears... I can't start again, I can't waste these cigarettes, they are unobtainable here, and Papa can't do without them.

My father takes a postcard out of a drawer in his desk and hands it to me. On it I see the dark head of a little girl emerging from a big bunch of roses... "Look what's written on the other side..." I recognize my Uncle Yasha's handwriting, I read: "My dearest little Tashok," and other affectionate words... And all sorts of images of him come into my head, there must have been a lot of them at that time, one of them, in any case, comes back to me now, the only one that has remained, which is always there...

He is walking with me, holding my hand, he is slim, like Papa, but taller and younger... he has come to fetch me from the rue Flatters, *he* meets Mama, and he even exchanges a few words with her... We cross the big square outside the Petit Luxembourg gardens... and just before we go through the gate, he stops, lets go of my hand, bends over me, takes off his glove and clumsily buttons up the collar of my long grey overcoat with a cape... he looks at me... his eyes are very like Papa's, but they are less piercing, more gentle... from his narrow, pale face, from his gestures, something tender and gentle flows over me...

"This postcard was found on him..." My father doesn't

need to say any more, I know that my uncle is dead, he was asphyxiated in the cabin of the boat taking him from Sweden to Antwerp, where my father was waiting to meet him... It was to prevent his brother being handed over to the *Okhrana*, a terrifying name that I have learnt here, that my father had to leave Russia for ever... Papa has taken the postcard back... "Aren't you going to give it to me?"... "No, I wanted you to see it, but I'll keep it for you..." I feel like crying, it seems to me that he, too, wants to cry, I would like to throw myself in his arms, hug him, but I don't dare... Here, he isn't the same as he used to be... he is distant, withdrawn...

—He never called you Tashok any more...

—It took me quite a while to notice that... All I felt at that time, I think, was a sort of reserve, of embarrassment in him, especially when Vera was present, and she almost always was. But even at a moment like this, when we are alone, Papa and I, with such a strong bond between us, between us alone, the embarrassment subsists.

All right then, since Vera has refused to buy me one, in a single second, my decision has been made... I lag behind, I stretch out my hand, I grab one of the little sachets of sugared almonds piled up in the window of a confectionery, I hide it in my wide jacket with the sailor collar, and I join Vera, with one hand propping the sachet up against my stomach... But very soon they catch up with us... the sales assistant has seen me through the window... "The little girl has just stolen a sachet of sugared almonds..." Vera glares at her, her eyes dilate, become an intense blue... "What's that you're saying? That's impossible!" And I shake my head automatically, I say No! without conviction... the assistant points or merely looks at the bulge at the bottom of my jacket, and that's enough, I bring out the sachet, passing it under the elastic waistband, and I hold it out... Without a word, we follow Vera, who goes back to the shop, crosses it, goes to the far end where the cash desk is, apologizes, and pays for the sachet... The cashier sympathizes... "Ah, Madame, children nowadays..." The assistant wants to give her the parcel, but Vera stops her... "No, thank you..." She refuses to take it.

We go out, we go back to the house... I don't remember

how... not speaking, or, at least, certainly not about what has just happened.

Vera refrains, with that obstinacy that nothing can overcome when she has made a decision, from taking any part in my education. I think this must be the result of discussions between her and my father... I have never heard them, but I have a suspicion that my father has criticized her concerning me...

—Even though you never complained...

—I never said a word to him about Vera.

—Why, I wonder... you weren't afraid of her...

—No... But it is curious... in a certain way, I felt I was on equal terms with her.

—It was rather, don't you think, that you were afraid of upsetting your father...

—Perhaps... I had the impression that he wasn't happy, he seemed worried... there was something about him that made me want to protect him...

On our return, nothing was said in my presence, but I knew that Vera would tell him, indignantly... and I wondered whether my father wouldn't criticize her for having refused me... *he* certainly wouldn't have done so, and then it wouldn't have happened...

That was what I was saying to myself, I think, when, as always, shortly after dinner, I went to my room, Vera to hers, and my father to his study...

I am in bed, I'm just going to sleep, when my father comes in, looking angry... "How could you have done such a thing?... Do you realize what a situation you put Vera in... and you yourself... it's disgraceful..." I feel that he's tired, that it's a real ordeal for him to look angry, he starts walking up and down in my room, I feel he's trying to work himself up... "It's incredible! such dishonesty, such deception..." He stops by my bed... "But for goodness' sake, what came over you?" "It was because I wanted them so much..." With this answer I give him, without meaning to, the impetus, the force he lacks...

—Without meaning to, certainly. Your solicitude for him didn't go *that* far...

—These words make him furious... He repeats them: "Because I wanted them! I wanted them! So I allow myself no matter what. So I get caught like a thief, I injure other people... I want them, well then, I do everything that comes into my head... Can you beat it, I want them..." it seems to me that now he really is suffering and in a rage... "What about me, then, do you imagine that I do everything I want? What do you think, then?... I want them so much that nothing restrains me, nothing counts..." These furious words traverse me and go somewhere else, somewhere beyond me... "Ah, when one has such a nature..." now I feel his disgust reaching me... and I can even say, I'm not exaggerating... his hatred... So I turn over towards the wall... He says some more words like... Things will come to a pretty pass later, they bode well, we shall see some splendid results... and he goes out, closing the door angrily.

I'm not doing anything, I'm daydreaming, sitting at a big wrought iron table in a parched garden, probably that of a villa on the outskirts of Paris, is it Clamart or Meudon? where we are spending the summer. Adèle, who has come from Brittany to look after Lili, is sitting opposite me quite near the table, her head bent over her needlework or embroidery. Her face is lined and greyish, her hair, drawn back into a little bun at the nape of her neck, is greying, she is wearing, as always, a long grey dress, her nose is curved like a beak, a corner of her wrinkled eyelid droops over her eye... like certain birds of prey... but she hasn't the intimidating look they have when they perch immobile, somnolent, in their big cages. She is very lively and active, and I have never discovered anything spiteful in her... nor anything good, it's as if she can't have any feelings.

While she sews or embroiders, she asks me to pass her the scissors, which are near me on the table. I pick them up absent-mindedly by the end nearest to me and hand them to her... She has raised her head, her completely expressionless, beady little black eyes stare at the steel point aiming at her, and these words emerge from her pinched lips: "Didn't anyone teach you, then, at your mother's place, that that isn't the way to pass scissors?"

I am perfectly well aware of the proper way to pass pointed objects like scissors and knives, but "at your mother's place" blocks the words that were about to rise in me: "Oh, I'm sorry."

"At your mother's place..." when I have never heard anyone make the slightest allusion to my mother in front of Adèle. Never anything that might have made me think that Adèle knew of her existence. And now it seems that not only does she know of the existence of my mother, but she never lets my mother out of her sight... she sees her through me... she still sees her mark on me. Signs that I carry unwittingly... bad signs.

—Negative ones... Yes, negative in you, whereas those same signs in other people are positive... In you, the signs are reversed. That's why both Adèle and Vera say of you, with a certain note of scorn... "Oh, she isn't difficult, she'll eat anything," which implies that Lili's continual rejection of food and her whims and caprices are the sign of a sensitive temperament... As, moreover, her delicate health is a quality, while your good health is the mark of a rather coarse, crude nature.

And also the word "nervous," applied to Lili, takes on a positive meaning... "She's nervous" means: "What vital force she has, how lively she is!"

—All this ought to have made me guess what I was in Adèle's eyes, what, as the perfect servant, she had very soon

141

grasped... This was the sort of thing that she understood immediately, that she must have been saying to herself when, raising and wrinkling the skin of one of her thin cheeks, she expelled some air between her side teeth with a little click which seemed to mean: "I know a thing or two... I know life. I'm not easily taken in. Ah, what can you expect, that's the way it is..." and she accompanied these reflections, generally expressed by her little click, with a nod of the head and an "Ah, Lord save us... Ah Lord, yes" which indicated certitude. There was no possible doubt. The moment she arrived she had sniffed out the atmosphere of the house, she had smelt "which way the wind blew," she knew where there was strength and where there was weakness. And which one was Madame's child and which was the child of a woman for whom Madame has no great liking, against whom Madame bears a grudge, a child to whom, if you happen to feel like it, you have every right to say, not even out of spite, but because that's the way it is, Ah Lord, it can't be helped... in those parts, where this child comes from, they don't know about these things, they know nothing of such refinements... "Didn't anyone teach you, then, at your mother's place, the proper way to pass scissors?"

I isn't easy to understand where you got it from... how it was, as never before—never when you were preparing for the Brébants' school—you felt such elation, such impatience...

—It certainly wasn't from what my father's friend said in front of me... "You simply must send her to the local primary school. Their teaching can't be bettered. A solid groundwork that lasts a lifetime..." I remember their every word, but that wasn't enough, at ten, I wasn't a sufficiently reasonable little monster...

—No, that can't explain the strange attraction I felt towards that forbidding-looking school in the rue d'Alésia. Its dusty brick walls were like those of the school in the rue des Feuillantines, they were just as dreary, just as bleak.

—From my room, which overlooked a courtyard adjacent to the playground, I could hear the children shouting and screaming, they must have been let out, as we were in those days, into an enclosure covered with gravel, or cement, without a single tree... and then, when the whistle blew, it was like an abrupt fall, like a sudden loss of consciousness, that total silence.

But while I watch Vera spreading a big sheet of navy blue paper over the table, opening at their middle the books and exercise books, arranging them on the sheet in all directions, changing their place, calculating, considering, and then cutting, folding, closing, smoothing, pressing and, finally, contemplating... she has her young, animated look, she seems to like doing this better than filling cigarettes... what I feel as I watch her is similar to the happy excitement I had felt when I was watching how they cut out, rolled up, stuck, painted, tied with golden thread, put ribbons around the objects that were going to decorate the Christmas tree.

I don't ask Vera to let me help her, I can see that it's too complicated, I don't want to spoil anything, but she does let me take a bit of cotton wool dipped in a little water in a saucer and stick a big, white, blue-edged label in the precise middle of each book. And then, with my new red pen with a new nib in the end of it I trace, in my very best handwriting, at the top of the label: Nathalie *Ꞇ*cherniak...

—How is it that this elaborate *Ꞇ* has suddenly come back to you from so long ago, when later you always wrote your name with a T like the printed character...

—I can see it again now, that quaint old *Ꞇ* which had completely vanished. I only adopted the other one, the very simple one, composed of two strokes, when I went to the lycée. I considered it newer, rather daring...

—Do you remember how Vera, when she saw that T one day, said to you... "Goodness, that's much nicer... Where did you get that idea from? I'm going to write it like that, too..." and that almost admiring approbation from Vera... it was so rare...

—It left me quite amazed, very flattered.

Every morning at the same time, before he shut the front door behind him, my father used to call out to no one in particular: "I've gone." Not "I'm going," but "I've gone"... as if he was afraid of being kept back, as if he already wanted to be a long way from here, over there, in his other life. And I, too, used to hurl myself out of doors with the same impatience...

—But you didn't compare yourself to him...

—I didn't compare myself to anyone. I'm just trying to rediscover, through what I perceived in him, what was going on in me when, schoolbag in hand, I rushed down the stairs and ran to school...

The vague smell of disinfectant, the cement staircases, the classrooms grouped around a treeless courtyard, their high, dirty beige walls, with no other adornment than the blackboard at the rear of the dais and a drab map of the French departments, all this radiated something which, the moment I went in, gave me a feeling, a presentiment, of a life...

—A more intense life?

—"More" isn't the right word. "Different" would be better. A different life. No comparison between the life I have left behind me there, outside, and this completely new life... But how, but where can I grasp it, so as to bring it back just a little, that new life, my real life...

—Be careful, or you'll be getting pretentious...

—Right, then let us simply try first to isolate one of those moments... in it alone... let me say this... so many pleasures jostle one another...

A little cramped in my thick, black, long-sleeved overalls that fasten at the back, not easy to button, I lean over my desk as do the other girls in my class, all about the same height and age as me... we are writing on a sheet of paper, at the top left of which each of us has first put her surname and first name, at the top right the date, and in the middle the word "Dictation" which, as with the name and the date, has to be underlined, by skillfully sliding a pen along a ruler without making any smudges. The line must be perfectly straight and clear.

147

The mistress walks up and down the rows between the desks, her voice rings out clearly, she articulates every word very distinctly, sometimes she even cheats a bit by purposely accentuating a liaison, to help us, to enable us to hear what letter such and such a word ends with. The words in the dictation seem to be words chosen for their beauty, for their perfect purity. Each one stands out distinctly, its shape becomes apparent, unlike that of any word in my books... and then, with ease, with natural elegance, it attaches itself to the word that precedes it and to the one that follows it... you have to be very careful not to spoil them... I feel a little apprehensive while I search... this word I'm writing, is it really identical with the one which I've already seen, which I know? Yes, I think so... but should it end in "ent"? Careful, it's a verb... remember the rule... is it certain that the word down there is really its subject? Look carefully, don't let anything escape you... there is nothing in me now, other than what is striving, searching, hesitating, returning, finding, isolating, inspecting... yes, that's it, that really is the subject, it's in the plural, so it has to end in an "s," and that means I have to put "ent" at the end of that verb...

My satisfaction, my relief, are quickly followed by a new anxiety, once again I strain every nerve... what game can be more exciting?

The mistress collects our papers. She is going to examine them, indicate the mistakes in red ink in the margin, then count them up and give the work a mark. Nothing can equal the fairness of the mark she will write under my name. It is justice itself, it is equity. It alone gives rise to that trace of approbation on the mistress's face when she looks at me. I am nothing other than what I have written. Nothing that I don't know, that people project on to me, that they foist on to me without my knowledge, as they are always doing there, outside, in my other life... I am completely protected from whims and caprices, from obscure, disturbing movements, suddenly provoked... is it by me? or is it by what they perceive behind me and which I mask? And also, nothing reaches me here of that love, "our love," as Mama calls it in her letters... which gives rise to something in me that hurts, which, in spite of the pain, I am supposed to cultivate, to nurture, and which, ignobly, I try to stifle... No trace of all that here. Here, I am in security.

Laws, which everyone has to respect, protect me. Everything that happens to me here can only depend on me. I am responsible for it. And the only aim of the solicitude, the concern which surrounds me here, is to help me to possess, to accomplish, what I myself desire, what gives me, *me* first and foremost, such pleasure... "But Nathalie, what has happened to you again with the verb *apercevoir*? You've given it two 'p's again!" "Oh, how could I have?... it was because I was thinking about *apparaître* again"... "Listen, my dear, you know what you are going to do, you're going to write out twenty times: *Je n'aperçois qu'un 'p' au verbe apercevoir.*" And I admire such ingenuity.

It's "for my good," like everything we do here, that they try to put into my mind exactly what is made to its measure, especially designed for it...

—Not altogether, though... often it seems difficult to grasp, a bit too elaborate or too vast...

—Yes, just sufficiently so to stop my mind slacking, going soft, to oblige it to extend itself as far as possible and make room for what is presented to it, for what it is supposed to be filled with... the numbers in the multiplication table, or the names of the French departments, and then, those of the prefectures, and then, one more effort, to get it to find room for the names of the subprefectures to establish themselves in it... here they are at last, in their proper place... they obey my summons, all I have to do is say the name of a department and immediately, obediently, the names of the prefectures and subprefectures present themselves, one after the other... Only perfect mastery can give such satisfaction.

Even there, outside, school protects me. People pass by on the other side of my door without stopping, they let me work...

But I, on the other hand, am always allowed to go into my father's study when he has come home and is resting in his dark green leather armchair, with his legs outstretched, after the long days he spends on his feet at his test tubes and retorts... but he says that while he is working he never feels tired... He immediately puts down the chemistry magazines he is looking through or his fat evening paper... He looks at the exercise book I have in my hand...

—It was when you were in the class that prepared you for the primary school leaving certificate that you took him problems which didn't really seem designed for your mind.

—However hard I tried to remember the proper way to work it out, I couldn't manage to discover the number of litres of water that poured out of taps, or those terrible arrival times of trains that pass one another... My father found these numbers in an instant by the mysterious, miraculous procedure of algebra... "This is what the answer must be... But you have to find it by arithmetic... And I was never taught that." So here we are, the two of us, straining every nerve, my father sitting by my side at his desk, and me trying to remember what the mistress had explained... which I thought I had remembered but which has escaped me... sometimes, with our combined forces, our reasoning leads us to the number, that's it, it's the one my father arrived at through algebra. We are both filled with the same satisfaction, it relaxes us, is visible on our faces as we go into the dining room, sit down at the table and, without another word about our problem, eat our meal with the others.

But sometimes, we haven't found the answer, and after dinner we start looking for it again.

—It sometimes happened that your father finally told you that you must go to bed... he'd go and ask the help of one or other of his friends who lived nearby... "*He* will know, he knows more than I do about these things... But what an idea to get children to solve such problems!"

—I am almost or even completely asleep when Papa comes in... "Are you asleep?" "No, it's all right... Have they done it, then?" "Yes, it's very simple, how is it we didn't think of it?" Papa sits down near me on my bed and explains... It doesn't seem so simple to me... it's floating... muddled... then suddenly, it divides into very distinct elements which, almost of their own accord, fall into place, into their proper place... there can't be any other... in impeccable order, they succeed one another until they get to the number that is waiting for them, which is the indubitable sign of their fulfilment... "I'll write it down at once." "Quickly, then, hurry up, it's late."

I no longer remember where this took place... through the enveloping haze, I can only discern the very vague figure of my father sitting by my side. I rather think he is in profile, he doesn't look at me when he announces, in I have forgotten what terms, that my mother is offering to take me back.

—After a year and a half... or perhaps two years...

—He tells me that she is making one condition: she won't be able to come herself or to send anyone to fetch me, he will have to take it upon himself to send me to her... And he knows perfectly well that if she is really so keen, she can quite well, she can afford it... and, for his part, this time he won't lift a little finger to help her, unless... "Unless *you* ask me to..."

It isn't difficult to reconstruct what must have filled the silence that preceded my reply: the shock caused by this abrupt reappearance of what I had been wrested away from, which I had made an effort to put out of my mind, which the letters that came from there, more and more remote, almost unreal, had helped to distance... then, under this brutal rapprochement, the discovery of a new distancing... and then, the burden my father is laying on me, the responsibility for this decision, which I alone must take... and what else, that is equally plausible?... but this reconstitution of what I must have felt is like a cardboard model that reproduces on a small scale what the buildings, houses, temples, streets, squares and gardens of a submerged town must have been like...

—Not altogether...

—Something still arises, as real as ever, an enormous mass... the impossibility of wresting myself away from what has such a strong hold on me, I have embedded myself in it, it supports me, sustains me, hardens me, shapes me... Every day it gives me the feeling that I am climbing to a culminating point in myself, where the air is pure, invigorating... a peak from where, if I am able to reach it, to keep myself on it, I shall see the whole world stretching out in front of me... nothing will be able to escape me, there will be nothing I shan't manage to know...

—It's curious that you should have experienced precisely the feeling that primary school teaching sought to provide...

—I was astonished when I discovered much later that

that was indeed one of the aims of their teaching. In any case, with me it succeeded.

—School dominated your existence... it gave it a meaning, its true meaning, its importance... When you felt so ill, you had measles, you prayed to Heaven...

—Yes, it's comic, I entreated it to let me go on living until "I knew everything"...

—And how it threw you, how it confused you when, later, at the lycée, you discovered that that apparently finite, entirely accessible world, was opening out on all sides, coming apart, disintegrating...

—But to come back to my reply, I didn't keep him waiting long... just long enough for a slight recoil... it will be painful for me to be the one to sever the bond that still attaches me to my mother, it is no longer very strong, but at certain moments I feel it, it starts tugging at me... a pain like those latent ones that are revived by the surrounding atmosphere, cold, humidity... but my father's words... "If she is really so keen, she can quite well..." act like an anaesthetic that helps me to complete, without suffering too much, the extraction of what is still clinging... ah, I've done it, "I want to stay here."

I don't know whether my father took me in his arms, I don't think so, that wouldn't have made me feel any more strongly the force of what unites us, and his total, unconditional support, nothing is demanded of me in exchange, no word must go and convey to him what I feel... and even if I didn't feel for him what other people call love, but which between him and me is not given a name, that wouldn't make any difference, my life would be just as essential to him... perhaps more so?... as his own... At all events, equally so.

I knew that in the joy he was restraining there was also the certainty that I had made the right choice for myself.

—But for himself... had he thought of that? it's obvious that your presence in his household could only make his life more difficult... It came out later that before he made the decision to remarry he had asked your mother whether she would agree to let you stay with him, and that she hadn't even deigned to reply...

—How can one know whether a feeling of bitterness hadn't crept into him... but the only thing I noticed was his relieved, relaxed air, and a joyful complicity with me that I can still hear in his voice when he said: "You know, all I have to do is make no move... If I don't send you there myself, there's no risk of anyone coming to take you back."

On Wednesday afternoons when I come out of school, since there is no homework to be done for the next day, I sometimes go to play with Lucienne Panhard, a girl in my class. She is the same age as me, give or take a couple of months, and the same height, her thin face is very gay, her eyes are slightly slanting, and her two thick golden plaits, which her mother takes a long time braiding, come down to below her waist, not like my two "rats' tails" which only reach my shoulders and which I can myself plait very quickly. Lucienne waits for me at the corner of the rue d'Alésia and the rue Marguerin, while I run and leave my schoolbag and tell them I'm going to play with her.

Her parents' café, with "Panhard" written in big red letters above the door, is right at the end of the avenue du Parc Montsouris, just by the entrance to the park, on the right, at the corner of the two streets.

I like this very bright, well-polished little café, Lucienne's parents seem young and kind, they laugh a lot, they joke... I am pleased when Madame Panhard allows us to wash the cups and glasses, this is a favor for which we have to ask her permission, promising to be very careful... But what I like best is putting down a glass of wine or a cup of coffee on the little tables in front of the customers, saying "Voici, Madame," in the tone of a real waitress, picking up the coins, "Merci, Monsieur," taking them back to the cash desk, watching to see the customers leave and then rushing up, clearing the table, wiping it thoroughly with a damp sponge. I don't know whether it is that my zeal, my amusement, are communicated to Lucienne, but, even though she can have this good fortune every day, she is just as intent as I am to see that we take turns to do the serving... customers sitting at the tables are rare at this time of day, we fight over them, sometimes Madame Panhard intervenes, she chooses between our outstretched hands, she dismisses one pair... "No, it isn't your turn this time..." she puts the coveted glass or cup into the other pair... "Here, take this, it's your turn... And it will be yours next time..." For our tea, she lets us choose a croissant or a brioche or a madeleine from under the domed glass dish-cover, she gives us each a bar of chocolate and pours us each a glass of lemonade, which we drink standing at the counter... When we've had enough of playing at being dishwashers or waitresses we go into the park, near the entrance, we skip, whirling the rope round as fast as we can, we catch a little rubber ball, which we throw up higher and higher into the air, we try to juggle with two, then three, balls.

We don't talk to each other very much, and I don't know why it is that I'm never bored with her, nor she, I think, with me.

It's the recitation lesson... I watch the mistress's hand, her pen is running down the list of names... pausing... couldn't she go a little farther, as far as the letter T?... she gets there, her hand stops, she raises her head, her eyes seek me out, she calls me...

I like to feel that slight fear, that excitement... I know the text very well by heart, I'm not likely to make a mistake, to forget a single word, but the most important thing is for me to start off in the right tone of voice... there, I've started... mustn't let my voice go too high, too low, mustn't force it, mustn't make it vibrate, that would make me feel ashamed... my voice rings out in the silence, the words come out very clearly, exactly as they should, they carry me away, I melt into them, my feeling of satisfaction...

—No actress can have experienced it more intensely...

—None. Even though there is no applause, but what applause, what ovation, can give more joy than the joy I feel through the certainty of having reached perfection... which is confirmed, as is only right and proper, by the mistress when she pronounces these words, which leave no room for the slightest reservation: "That is very good. I will give you ten out of ten."

*T*yebya podbrossili... this is one of the rare occasions when I can remember which language Vera used in talking to me, she sometimes spoke French with me, and always with Lili so as not to "confuse the child with two languages"... but this time I do know, she said it to me in Russian... in French she would have had to say *on t'a abandonnée*, which would be a very feeble, anaemic equivalent of the Russian words... the Russian verb she used...

—But where was it? Apropos of what?

—We were walking side by side in a dreary garden, along a sandy path winding between the lawns... it can only have been the parc Montsouris... Vera, very thin and pale, wearing a big brown velvet hat, a boa round her neck, was pushing Lili's pram, when she said to me: "*Tyebya podbrossili*"... But apropos of what? that, I can't remember... perhaps apropos of nothing at all, just like that, because it suddenly crossed her mind... she didn't try to keep it there, or she couldn't... the Russian words came out hard and harsh, as they always did from her mouth... *podbrossili*, a verb whose literal meaning is "to throw out" but which also has an irreplaceable prefix which means "under," "from below," and this ensemble, that verb and its prefix, conjure up a picture of a burden that someone has surreptitiously unloaded on to someone else...

—As the cuckoo does?

—Yes, but it seems to me that in the cuckoo's act there is caution, foresight, whereas that Russian word conjures up a brutal, and at the same time underhand, rejection...

—You certainly weren't interested, at that moment, in discovering all the hidden riches of that word...

—I didn't marvel at them, as I do now, but what is quite certain is that I didn't lose an atom... what child would have?... of all that that verb, and the personal pronoun preceding it: *tyebya podbrossili*, conveyed to me...
And curiously enough, at the same time as Vera's resentment against the people who had unloaded this burden on to her and obliged her to take it on, at the same time as her rage against the liability that I was to her... yes, at the same time as these words hurt me, their very brutality brought me reassurance... They don't want me there, they reject me, so it isn't my fault, it wasn't *my* decision, I have to stay

here whether I like it or not, I have no choice. It is clear, it is certain, that it is here and nowhere else that I must live. Here. With everything that "here" contains.

—And you already knew that Vera's character, her relations with you, were only a part, and not the most important one, of that "everything."

When I go into my room, even before I have put my schoolbag down, I see that my bear, Mishka, whom I left lying on my bed... he is softer and more cuddly than he has ever been, when it's cold I cover him up to his neck with a little knitted woolen square so that all you can see is his silky little yellow head, his limp ears, the worn, black threads of his muzzle, his shiny eyes, which are still as lively... he's gone... but where is he? I rush out... "Adèle, my bear has disappeared." "Lili took it"... "But how is that possible?" "She managed to walk as far as your room... the door was open..." "Where is he? Where did she put him?" "Ah, she tore it to bits, that wasn't difficult, it was falling apart anyway, it was just an old rag..." "But he can be mended..." "No, there was nothing to be done, I threw it away..."

I don't want to see him again. I mustn't say another word, if I do, Adèle is sure to reply: Bears like that can be found anywhere, and brand new ones, much nicer ones... I run into my room, throw myself on to my bed and cry my eyes out...

—You have never resented anyone as you resented Lili at that moment.

—After that I put everything out of her reach, the Russian carved wood boxes, the round one and the rectangular one, the painted wooden bowl, and I don't know what other treasures, *my* treasures, no one else knows their value, they mustn't be touched, appropriated by that squalling, frantic, insensitive, evil little creature, that devil, that demon...

I ask Vera, I have forgotten in what context, but it isn't important: "Why mustn't I do that?" and she answers: "Because it isn't done," in her stubborn, inscrutable tone, compressing the vowels even more than she usually does, the consonants collide with one another and pour out in a hard, harsh jet that lapidates everything stirring in me, wanting to surface...

"Because it isn't done" is a barrier, a brick wall which she drags me up against, against which we stumble... our vacant, globular eyes stare at it, we can't get over it, it's useless to try, our resigned heads turn away from it.

—At such a moment, didn't it occur to you to use what your mother had given you before she left you... you had kept it for quite a time...

—Yes, those words of Mama's in the hotel room in Berlin, the evening before our separation: "Vera is stupid"... a parcel she gave me to take with me, like the ones you give your child when you are sending it to boarding school... Here, my darling, you may find this useful when you're away from me, you may need it there...

—No, here I must stop you, you're letting yourself be carried away, your mother never dreamed of giving you that like the "tuck," or the cough and cold cures children going to boarding school are provided with... It was you who forced her hand by your questions: "What was it Uncle said to you, Mama? Who was he talking about?" It was because she finally gave in to you that she answered: "Uncle told me that Vera is stupid"... but while she was saying those words she had lost sight of you, she wasn't seeing you, it wasn't you she was thinking of, but something that had made her look surprised and amused... something funny the uncle had confided to her which she had considered for an instant... that was how, with her invariable insouciance and thoughtlessness, not considering what use you might put it to, she let you take and carry away with you: "Vera is stupid."

—And at first, I kept it, it was well worthwhile, I had never known anything like it. A grown-up rigged out in an invisible dunce's cap... It's clear that my father doesn't know it, nor Vera herself, nor anyone else, except me and the uncle who sometimes comes to see them—her and Papa—as if nothing had happened, and he never shows the slightest sign of anything.

"Vera is stupid"... this means that something must be missing in her head, and the poor woman doesn't realize it, there's nothing to be done, she's just made that way... but from the outside, what do you recognize it by? What does Uncle see? He talks to her exactly as he does to everyone else... but for my part, when she forbids me or advises me to do this or that... when she says what she thinks about whatever it may be... is she capable of thinking? can she understand? since she is "stupid."

It's a nuisance not to be able to rely on what she tells me, always to be obliged to question myself, and there is no one I can confide in. To whom can you reveal such things?

—I have a feeling that one day, shortly after your arrival, before Lili was born, when she was looking after you to the best of her ability... did I dream it? is it possible that you finally burst into tears and told her...

—It's barely believable, but I can see it... I have thought over, as best I can, what Vera has just asked me to do, since I can't possibly believe everything she tells me, I decided that she wasn't right, so I refused to listen to her...

—But what could it have been?

—I don't know, all I can remember is my despair, my solitude, that enormous weight I must free myself from... she questions me, she doesn't understand... "Why are you so stubborn? Why do you refuse to listen to me?"... "I can't say it..." "Yes, you can... go on, say it..." "No, I can't"... and finally, between my sobs... "I can't listen to you because... because... you... are... stupid... Someone told me that..." "But who?" I don't know how long it took for those words which were choking me to force their way out and explode in her face: "It was the uncle who came to fetch me in Berlin... he said that to Mama."

As improbable as it may seem, it is unfortunately certain that it did take place. But this was at the beginning of my stay in Paris, when I was still that unsteady, fledgling child who had barely grown out of "its ideas," who clung, confided, confessed, risked being exasperating, provoking resentment and hostility, so as not to remain alone, apart, carrying within itself something which it must let no one see, but which is sapping its strength, taking possession of it...

But I have been here for nearly two years now, I am no longer that crazy child... The words "Vera is stupid" don't come back to me any more... And anyway, there is no word to apply to her...

—When you come to think of it, you never did apply any word to her. Not even "unkind"...

—It's odd... when I happened to hear other children saying that my stepmother was unkind, it surprised me... other images immediately came to mind which had nothing to do with "unkind"...

At all events, when she said to me, and she must have said it more than once, "Because it isn't done"... "Vera is stupid" wasn't like one of those antibodies that enable the organism to defend itself against an invasion by microbes. No, in that case, "Vera is stupid," even if I had had it at my disposal, wouldn't have been of any use to me as an antidote.

I had touched on something which she had once and for all forbidden herself to approach, she isn't as stupid as all that, she has no time to waste.

"It isn't done" cuts short all examination, makes all discussion useless.

"It isn't done" is like the ancient Oriental emperors, before whom their subjects bow, without ever daring to raise their eyes up to their faces.

And *I* had had the presumption to want to observe from close up, to touch... what is there to stop me?... Why can't I do that? And the thing that had allowed these absurd, indecent words to take shape in my mind, to grow, to stir, to show themselves, had received a sharp, well-aimed blow with a ruler: "Because it isn't done."

A well-deserved blow, when one was foolish enough, presumptuous enough to want an explanation, to want to understand... and, why not, to judge?... or even, if the explanation doesn't seem satisfactory, to go and do, in the face of the whole world, something that isn't done?

When you have been bludgeoned with "Because it isn't done," you are... I was going to say stunned, bemused... that's what anyone might think, but in actual fact, I was filled with impotent rage which made me writhe, squirm... the blind, absurd fury aroused by an object you have come into sharp collision with, you want to hit back at it, I wanted to belabour it, to trounce it. But to return blow for blow and bludgeon "Because it isn't done" with: "And why not? Why isn't it done"... No, I couldn't do that, I wasn't brave enough...

—And yet the risk, seen from the outside, wasn't very great...

—But, on the other hand, what those words might have provoked inside Vera... that silent explosion, that furious seething, those acrid vapours, those incandescent avalanches... I never deliberately dared to trigger that off, never, even under my breath, even in a whisper, did I allow to reach her ears: "And why isn't that done?"

When friends come, my father is transformed. He no longer seems withdrawn, he relaxes, he becomes animated, he talks a lot, he argues, he evokes memories, he tells anecdotes, he enjoys himself, and he likes to make the others enjoy themselves. Everyone sitting around him at the big oval dining room table looks at him with cordiality, with admiration, he is so witty, so intelligent... even Mama once said to me, and this is one of the rare remarks I ever heard her make about him... "Your father is very intelligent..."

—She said that, apropos of nothing in particular, one day in St. Petersburg, in a detached, indifferent tone of voice, as if she was making a simple observation to which she didn't attach any great importance...

—If it is a Sunday afternoon, Misha is there with me, his parents are there too, and Monsieur and Madame Pereverzev, Monsieur Ivanov, a great friend of my father, and Monsieur Bilit—who is in the habit of turning up unexpectedly in the evening of any day of the week, and if it happens to be dinner time they lay an extra place for him—and Vera, who, amazed and amused by his insatiable appetite, even if the meal is quite copious, has his favourite dish made for his dessert, a jam omelette. Monsieur Bilit is very good at mathematics. He lost an arm, his left arm, I no longer remember in which uprising, in which attack, and a wooden hand in a brown leather glove protrudes from his sleeve. Two rather elderly sisters are there too, and other guests that I don't know so well, whom I remember less well.

When I look at those women and men sitting together round the table, aging people, rather melancholy and tired, I tell myself that no one would ever guess just how out of the common they are, extraordinary human beings, revolutionaries, heroes who have faced the most terrible dangers without flinching, who have stood up to the Tsar's police, thrown bombs... they have marched by stages, their feet in chains, to the wilds of Siberia, they have been locked up in dungeons, condemned to be hanged, and they have awaited death with serenity, preparing themselves—for when they would be at the foot of the gallows, when the executioner would come up to cover their heads in the dreadful hood, to put the slippery, soap-smeared rope round their necks—preparing themselves to shout for one last time: Long live the Revolution! Long live Liberty!

I feel an indiscriminate admiration for them all, but the one I like best, even more than Misha's parents and Monsieur and Madame Pereverzev, although I like them very much indeed, and often go to visit them, is Monsieur Ivanov.

You could say of his handsome face, with its fine features,

as, indeed, you could say of everything about him, that "it is the soul of goodness"... goodness radiates from the creases round his lips, from his light blue, faded eyes and even from the little bags under his eyes...

Monsieur Ivanov has a slight stammer, and this confers on him something even more gentle, something helpless, innocent... I have heard it said that his stammer began after they came to wake him in his condemned cell and told him that his sentence to be hanged had been commuted to life imprisonment. Naturally, he hadn't signed a petition for a pardon. Never, in spite of the entreaties of his parents and even the objurgations of the judges, did he agree to perpetrate such an act. Nor, moreover, would any of the people at that table have done so. When people say of someone in an undertone that he asked the Tsar to pardon him, it's as if they were revealing that he is secretly branded with some infamous mark.

Monsieur Ivanov was imprisoned in the Schlüsselburg fortress from the age of twenty until he was forty-five, for a long time in solitary confinement, with no other book to read than the Bible... I often hear these names: "Schlüsselburg fortress," "Peter and Paul fortress," "Okhrana," "The Black Hundreds"... and there is also a lot of talk about suspicious characters circulating in "The Colony," they pass themselves off as revolutionaries, but they may be secret agents of the police, spies... Misha sees them everywhere, and my father says, laughing, that Monsieur and Madame Agafonov have communicated their malady, "espionitis," to him...

—When, some years later, the revolution broke out and the dossiers of the Okhrana were opened, they saw that these suspicions were sometimes well-founded.

—My father, who makes fun of this malady, can't resist, when he dislikes someone, seizing on him and turning him into such a disconcerting, complicated and comic character that everyone listens as if fascinated, delighted by his humour, his strokes of inspiration, his sallies... his dark eyes sparkle, his white teeth glisten, his verve, his wit, are a glittering blade that cuts... sometimes into the quick... sometimes I feel that it reaches into me too... and yet it is into someone else, whom I know only slightly or not at all, that it plunges... but I feel its cold touch inside me... it hurts me a little, it frightens me a little... do the others feel it as I do? And Monsieur Ivanov? whose judgment, my father says, is so sound, so lucid? Does *he* think that my father is going too far... Up till now he has been smiling his calm, gentle smile... but now it's suddenly as if his smile has become a little frozen, there's a kind of movement in his eyes, it seems to me that something in him is contracting, retracting... but only very slightly... Someone gently stops my father... "There, I think, dear Ilya Evseitch, you are exaggerating a little... he isn't especially likeable, but I know him well, he isn't such a bad fellow..." As for Monsieur Ivanov, he just nods indulgently, he must look on these irrepressible outbursts of my father the way a grown-up watches the antics of a child, who is sometimes a little too turbulent, when he is amusing himself, getting excited... but he knows very well that he has a good heart, that he isn't malicious... he knows that even if the person my father has just so pitilessly portrayed were to come and ask him for help, he would immediately forget how he saw him, he would simply see before him a poor man in need, he wouldn't refuse him, he is

175

incapable of refusing...

—Vera sometimes tried to check him... "You give to anyone, people take advantage of you... I assure you that that
man is better off than you are..." and he would answer her,
slightly shrugging one shoulder... "Well, in that case, good
for him."

—Vera is sitting opposite my father, at the other side of
the table, in the place that belongs to the mistress of the
house, behind the big copper samovar. She pours the tea
into the cups and glasses, passes them round, takes them
back when they are empty, rinses out their dregs over a little
bowl placed under the tap, refills them, hands them round,
constantly watches everyone's plate, whatever happens no
one must lack anything... she never speaks, barely more
than a few words, or rather a few monosyllables, a few brief
laughs, to be polite... Does she even listen to what is being
said? Her staring, transparent eyes, which sometimes make
you think of cats' eyes, sometimes of those of wild animals,
occasionally focus on this or that face... and after the guests
have gone, she says, especially of someone who isn't an ha-
bitué, of a newcomer, in her brusque, unanswerable tone:
"So-and-so has a very good opinion of himself (or herself)."
You feel that that is a definitive statement, a condemnation
from which there is no appeal... and it always prompts the
same astonishment, the same questions in me: What on
earth is it that makes her recognize that? Why, out of so
many other judgments that you can make about people,
does she only ever make that particular one? And why does
she attach so much importance to it? It seems to me that

176

whatever they are like, she divides them into two categories: those who have a good opinion of themselves, and the rest.

—For a long time you didn't try to discover what that judgment might contain...

—It surprised me... It made me like them, made me a little envious of the ones "who had a good opinion of themselves"...

—Weren't they the ones who had been the most lively, the most interesting?

—That's probable... That curt "He (or she) has a good opinion of himself (or herself)," accompanied by that harsh little sound, km, km, that Vera made, after the guests had gone, gave the impression that she was blowing out a candle, a lamp...

All the chairs are empty, the lights have been put out, we can go to bed, we can finally relax...

This is the first time I have thought about it, it never occurred to me in those days, it seemed so natural, to go without saying, but what strikes me now is that no one made the slightest distinction between men and women, either from the intellectual or moral point of view. I had the feeling...

—Not even the feeling, you weren't even aware of...

—That's right, it was rather the absence of any sort of feeling of inequality.

—Vera had never taken part in any revolutionary action, but she had made great demands on herself and shown real bravery when she was a volunteer nurse during the war between Russia and Japan. Whenever my father referred to it, she became embarrassed and stopped him... "Oh, for goodness' sake, what are you saying? I only did what had to be done."

Going down the corridor past the door to Vera's bedroom, where she has gone to bed early, as she likes to do, "to read a good novel in peace," while my father stays a little longer in his study, reading chemistry magazines, making notes, I hear a strange sound... it isn't like anything I have ever heard before... it sounds like moans, like groans... or, perhaps, suppressed sobs... but there is something so defenceless, so innocent about it... it's like the distress, the despair of a child that escapes from him, he can't keep it back, it's wrung from the depths of his soul... it hurts just to hear it... I open the door, the light is on, Vera is lying in her bed, turned towards the wall, the sheets are pulled right up to her ears, all I can see is her dark brown hair, smoothed down for the night and drawn back over the nape of her neck into a plait which makes her look like a little girl...

I go up to her, I lean over the bed, I say very gently: "What's the matter? Don't you feel well?" I see her purplish, tear-stained, swollen face, the face of a big baby... "Can I help you? Would you like me to bring you a drink?"

She shakes her head, she manages to articulate: "It's nothing, it will pass"... I lift up a corner of the sheet, I wipe her face, I stroke her soft, silky, warm head, and she gradually calms down... Still without turning round, she brings out a hand, she puts it on mine, she presses my fingers... I ask her if she would like me to put the light out... "No no, don't bother, don't worry, it was nothing, I'm all right, I'll read a little longer..." And I go out, shutting the door quietly...

—Neither of you ever said a word about it later.

—And I never said a word about it to anyone.

Afterwards, I couldn't sleep, I was trying to understand... my father and Vera hadn't seemed to be on bad terms, which did sometimes happen, when their faces were frozen, when they barely spoke to one another at table... That evening they had seemed to be getting on well... so why? where had it come from?

And for the first time, I saw someone as familiar, as visible, as well-known as Vera was to me, becoming, under my very eyes, someone quite different... images, snatches of stories that seemed to have taken place at a distance from her, very far away, as if somewhere on the open sea, came back, stuck to her, covered her... She is very gay, affectionate, tender, even... her family, her friends love her as she deserves to be loved... she is always the first to want to enjoy herself, to suggest going off into the forest with a crowd of friends to pick wild strawberries, mushrooms, she is very good at finding them, at recognizing them... she adores dancing, no one waltzes better, no one dances the mazurka better than she does... sometimes they applaud her, she gets a prize... her dance cards, I've seen them in her drawers, with a blue or pink ribbon, are always full, all the dances have been engaged in advance... she fans herself as she throws back her face, so flushed, so pink, as in the old days when she danced with me in the rue Boissonade, she shakes her head, smiling... No, she can't, she has to refuse the next waltz to one of those superb officers in the white uniforms, whom I have admired when looking through her family album... there was also a photograph of her mother who has a very kind face, Vera loves her so much that she rarely lets a day go by without writing to her, and one of her brother, of her sister-in-law who is called Varya... Vera has no better friend than her... And she has left all that behind her, she is at the other end of the world... And yet I have never heard her regret it or complain, even when she came back after she had been to stay with her family in Moscow for a few days... The thing is that she is so resolute, so hard on herself... that big scar she has on her forearm, where at the age of fourteen she was bitten by a viper, she immediately sank her teeth into it, tearing out a bit of her own flesh to stop the poison from spreading... She must have softened a little this evening, weakened, and what she has left behind there must have come and invaded her, it filled her and poured out of her in groans, in tears...

And my father, too, is becoming transformed, he looks older to me, more sombre, more austere... she never addresses him by his first name... is it because she has too much respect for him? or is a little afraid of him? sometimes I have that impression... but why, I ask myself... and all these people here, people such as she has never seen, so different from the ones she has known... It is they who make her so stiff and mute when she's sitting behind the samovar, pouring out their tea, watching their plates... What are they saying? She doesn't listen, they aren't talking to *her*, they must be thinking that she... Of course, that's it... she must be imagining... while they go on talking among themselves, smiling at her, holding out their glasses and cups to her, bowing when they are given them, thanking her very politely, she is thinking that they find her...

—But there, I believe, you were mistaken, she wasn't thinking about herself, about the impression she was making on them... It was them alone she must have been seeing, those audacious people, never hesitating to give their opinion, to argue, sure of being well-educated and well-informed, so lucid, so intelligent, so fair, always on the right side...

—Yes, I see it now, that was what must have come into her mind, when, after they had gone, she said, as if she had noticed a peculiarity, a trait in them which made them laughable... "They have a good opinion of themselves."

"Describe your first sorrow. 'My First Sorrow' is the title of your next French essay."

—Didn't they rather call it "composition" in primary schools?

—Perhaps... at all events, that particular French composition, or essay, stands out from the rest. From the moment the mistress told us to write in our notebooks "My First Sorrow," it's impossible that I didn't have a presentiment... I wasn't often wrong... that this subject was a golden opportunity... I must have seen nuggets sparkling in a far-off mist... the promise of treasures...

I imagine that as soon as I could, I set off in search of them. I had no need to hurry, I had plenty of time, and yet I couldn't wait to find... everything would depend on it... What sorrow?...

—You didn't start by trying, searching through your own sorrows...

—To find one of my own sorrows? Of course not, goodness, what are you thinking about? One of my own real sorrows? that I had actually experienced... and besides, what could I call by that name? And which had been the first? I hadn't the slightest desire to ask myself... what I needed was a sorrow outside my own life, that I could consider while keeping myself at a safe distance... this would give me a sensation that I couldn't name, but I can feel it now just as I did then... a feeling...

—Of dignity, perhaps... that's what it might be called today... and also of domination, of power...

—And of liberty... I keep myself in the background, out of reach, I don't reveal anything that belongs only to me... but I prepare for other people something that I consider to be good for them, I choose what they like, what they might expect, one of those sorrows that suit them...

—And it was then that you were lucky enough to

glimpse... Where did you get it from?

—I have no idea, but the moment it appeared I felt a certainty, a satisfaction... I couldn't hope to find a nicer, more suitable sorrow... more presentable, more fascinating... the very model of a real first sorrow of a real child... the death of my little dog... what could be more imbued with childish purity, with innocence.

As improbable as it may seem, I did feel all that...

—But is it so improbable for a child of eleven, almost twelve... you were in the school leaving certificate class.

—This subject gave rise, as I expected, to a host of images, still succinct and vague, brief sketches... but which promised to become real beauties as they developed... On my birthday, oh what a surprise, I jump up and down and clap my hands, I throw myself on Papa's, on Mama's neck, a white ball in a basket, I press it to my heart, then our games, where though? but in a beautiful big garden, flowering meadows, lawns, it belongs to my grandparents, where my parents and my brothers and sisters spend their holidays... and then, the horror that will come... the white ball goes off towards the pond...

—The pond you had seen in a picture, bordered with

rushes, covered with water lilies...

—It has to be admitted that that is tempting, but here is something even more promising... the railway line... we're going for a walk near it, the little dog climbs up the embankment, I run after him, I call him, then here comes the train at full speed, the enormous, terrifying locomotive... this is a chance for splendours to be deployed...

The moment has come now... I keep delaying it... I'm afraid of starting off on the wrong foot, of not taking a proper run up to it... I start by writing the title... "My First Sorrow"... that might get me going...

The words I have settled on are not my everyday words, greyish words, barely visible, rather slovenly... *these* words are, as it were, beautifully dressed in their best clothes... most of them have come from places where good manners and brilliance are required... they have come from my anthologies, from dictations and also...

—Were they from books by René Boylesve, by André Theuriet, or was it already Pierre Loti?

—In any case, they are words whose origin guarantees elegance, grace, beauty... I enjoy their company, I have all the respect for them that they deserve, I see to it that nothing disfigures them... If I feel that something is spoiling their appearance, I immediately consult my Larousse, no nasty spelling mistake, no hideous pimple must blemish them.

And to connect them together, strict rules exist which you have to abide by... if I can't find them in my grammar book, if there is the slightest lingering doubt, it's better not to touch those words, to look for others which I can put in another phrase where they will be in their proper place, in their appropriate role. Even my own words, the ones I ordinarily use without really seeing them, when they have to come in here they acquire a respectable air, good manners, on contact with the others. Sometimes I slip in a rare word here or there, an ornament which will highlight the brilliance of the ensemble.

Often, the words guide me in my choice... thus, in this first sorrow, the "crisp rustle" of the autumn leaves that we crushed as we ran or as we rolled over on them—my little dog and I—had, after some hesitation, made me choose the autumn rather than the spring for our games in my grandparents' garden.

—And yet "the tender shoots and the downy buds" were pretty appealing...

—The autumn prevailed, and I didn't regret it... didn't I find there "the mellowness of the rays of a pale sun, the gold and purple leaves of the trees"...

Behind the closed door of my room, I am engaged in the most normal, the most legitimate, the most praiseworthy activity in the world, I am doing my homework. At this moment, it happens to be a French essay. I didn't choose the subject, it was given to me, even imposed on me, it's a subject made for me, within the capabilities of a child of my age... I am allowed to frolic within its limits, on a well-prepared, well-laid out ground, just as I am in the school playground or even, since these frolics are accompanied by great efforts, in the gymnasium.

Now the moment has come to concentrate all my forces for the great leap forward... the arrival of the train, its din, its scalding steam, its enormous, blazing eyes. And then, when the train has passed, between the rails the tuft of white hairs, the pool of blood...

But I won't let myself touch that yet, I want to let the words take their time, choose their moment, I know I can rely on them... the last words always make their appearance as if propelled by all the preceding ones...

In the darkness of the cinema in the rue d'Alésia, while I am watching goodness knows what silent film, accompanied by pleasant, exciting music, I call them up, or rather, I call them back, they have already come before, but I want to see them again... it's an opportune moment... I make them reverberate... should I change the place of that one?... I listen once again... really, the sentence they make unfolds and falls into place very nicely... still just a slight rearrangement perhaps... and then I must stop examining it, I might easily spoil it... I must just try to keep it as it is, word for word, until the moment comes to write it in my fair copy, beginning a new paragraph to make it stand out properly in all its beauty, and following it with the final full stop.

All I shall have to do then, is to judge the right distance underneath it and draw a nice straight line with my very clean pen and my ruler.

—Never, in the whole of your life, has any text you have

written given you such a feeling of satisfaction, of well-being...

Perhaps, later, another essay, the one on toys...

—A subject for a French essay in the third year at the lycée. The same impression of fulfilment, there too, when delightful words came to me, carrying "the fragrance of the past, of an odour of mildew that wafted up to my face when, alone in the attic of the old house, I had raised the heavy lid of the coffer in which abandoned, broken toys were lying pell-mell... a flood of charming memories..." I listened with enchantment to the faint murmur in my sentences of "a restrained melancholy, a touching nostalgia..."

—By this time, it was mostly from Balzac that words came to you... you have to agree that you hardly saw any difference between the quality of his texts, of those of Boylesve or Theuriet, and your own...

—And that resemblance brought me certainty, security... But I must admit that I found my own texts more delectable.

When I read over "My First Sorrow" one last time... I knew some of its passages by heart... I thought it perfect, very smooth, and clear, and well-rounded...

—You needed that clarity, that smooth roundness, you

didn't want anything to stand out...

—I liked things that were fixed, determinable, immutable... That was what delighted me later in plane geometry,
in inorganic chemistry, in the basic laws of physics... Archi-
medes' principle, Atwood's machine... no risk of seeing
anything whatsoever start to fluctuate, to become unstable,
uncertain... I was out of my depth the moment I had to
leave these regions where I felt perfectly secure and tackle
the shifting, disturbing ones of three-dimensional geometry,
of organic chemistry... "My First Sorrow" is as fixed and
rounded as one could wish, not the slightest asperity, no
abrupt, disconcerting movement... nothing but a slight,
regular swaying motion, a soft murmur...

Really, this essay deserves to be shown to my father. He
likes to look at my homework. Especially my French essays.

We have to be on our own. It is tacitly understood that
Vera must not be present. In the same way as it is agreed
between us, without a word having been spoken, that she
must never be there when I get my father to sign my school
report.

Of course, the cross the mistress pins on to my overalls,
and which I wear throughout the week, it's impossible to
prevent her seeing that, and for it not to give rise to something like little wavelets of displeasure, of hostility, in her.

When I go into my father's study with my essay in my
hand, he immediately abandons what he is doing and listens to me... and I , as I read to him, I rediscover the joys of
recitation, they are even increased... is there any other text
whose nuances my intonation can highlight better?

My father is always reserved, he doesn't spread himself in
a lot of compliments, but I don't need them, I know from

his expression, from the way he listens to me, that he is going to tell me it is very good. No more. But that is enough for me. Not for a second is there a question between us of any other kind of appraisal than he would make of my other homework. There is never even the remotest suggestion... the idea never even... of any "gift for writing"... nothing is farther...

—Are you sure?

—Absolutely. I have done no more than write a very good essay. I haven't taken any sort of liberties, and anyway, I have no wish to, I never try to exceed the limits assigned to me and go roaming God knows where, somewhere I have no business to be, looking for I don't know what... or rather, what my father hates more than anything, something he can never mention without contemptuously puckering his lips, screwing up his eyelids, and which he calls "vainglory"... certainly not, I am not looking for that. The idea of becoming a writer never occurs to me. Sometimes I wonder whether I couldn't become an actress... but for that you have to be as beautiful as Vera Koren or Robine. No, what I would like to be is a schoolteacher.

The day the mistress gives us back our essays, I wait with the presentiment, but it's more like the certainty, that the list will begin with my name. The mark written on the paper is less important... it will probably be an 8 or a 9... But, to confirm my success, it is absolutely necessary for my name to be at the head of the list!...

191

—Did it never occur to you that it would be the best of thirty rather mediocre essays, and that, consequently, that selection...

—No, never. For me, the number one represents an absolute. Something which nothing is superior to. It doesn't matter where. I have the illusion that it is beyond comparison. It isn't possible for what I have done to come after what anyone else has done.

—Your fury with yourself... it was at the lycée Fénelon... when for the first time Monsieur Georgin, giving back the Latin unseens, said to you: "But what has happened? You are..." was it third or second?...

—On my way home, I took the ignominious paper out of my schoolbag, I trampled on it, I tore it up, and I threw the scraps into the fountain in the place Médicis.

All the children I know say "Mama," Lili, too, can say it now, when Vera talks about me she always says my daughter... and people are sometimes amazed... You already have a daughter of that age? and it is true that she is only fifteen years older than I am... And then, even though she looks so young, it embarrasses me to call her Vera, as my father does, as if I were a grown-up, so one day I suggest to her... I have absolutely no recollection of how it happened... that I might call her Mama. She replies: "Certainly, but you will have to ask your mother's permission"...

I have, on the other hand, a perfect recollection of a particular meal, sitting between my father and Vera, of my tears falling into my soup and of the silence around me... my father doesn't ask any questions, he must know, Vera must have told him, the minute he got home she must have said: "Boretzkaya"... I know that that is how they refer to my mother when they are together, it comes from Kolya's surname... "Boretzkaya has replied... she doesn't agree..."

I try to hold back my tears, they flow faster and faster, I wipe them with my handkerchief, I blow my nose... my father has his irritated, angry look, his eyelids screwed up... he pats my shoulder for a second... "Don't upset yourself"... the expression he always used when he saw that I was "in a state"... "Don't upset yourself, it isn't worth it, I promise you." But he doesn't know what was in that letter... Mama's grief, indignation... it is heartless, insensitive, ungrateful, to forget the most sacred bonds, what should be dearest in the whole world, one's mother, a name that can be given to no other woman, out of the question even to say... this was the alternative I had suggested... "Mama-Vera." This name of Mama cannot be coupled to any other. I had only one mother on earth... and she wasn't dead yet...

My tears, the tears of former times, which for almost two years now had run dry... but how long the years were at that age... those tears return and are even more acrid, more corrosive.

I take some of the big sheets of blue paper which are used to cover my school books, and I cut out little squares, which I fold and refold in the way I have been taught, and make them into paper birds. On one side of each one's head, I write the surname, and on the other, the first name, of a pupil in my class: thirty in all and I am one of them. I arrange them on my table, side by side, in several rows, and I, their mistress... not the real one who is teaching us this year... a mistress I invent... I sit down on my chair facing them.

In this way, I can learn painlessly, and even enjoyably, the most deadly boring lessons. I have my history or geography book in front of me, and I put questions to my pupils and to myself... to the dunces, when I still don't know the lesson very well... they stammer, they say all sorts of stupid, funny things which I invent, imitating them... I love to imitate people, and often my imitations raise a laugh...

Dressed up in this fashion, in tomfoolery, clowning, comic absurdities, I manage to insert into myself and to retain things which, undisguised, would be rejected... peace treaties, names of battles, of towns, of departments, of countries, their surface area, the number of their inhabitants, their products... I sprinkle all that with whatever is to my taste... such as... "Tell me, yes, you, Madeleine Tamboitte... but don't look so bemused, for goodness' sake... *Who* won the battle of Poitiers? Who? Don't prompt her... I tap my pencil on my table impatiently... Who, did you say? *Charles et Marcel*... Bravo! No, don't laugh. It was Charles Martel, you ignorant girl... Char-les Mar-tel. And you, Suzanne Morin, tell me, *whom* did he repulse? What! the Germans! What on earth are you talking about, you pudding head... the Germans, they were the ones who took from us... tell us, Germaine Pelletier... and she answers in her high-pitched voice... Alsace-Lorraine, in 1870... Very good... And one day we are going to take it back. But in Poitiers..." "Madame!"... "Right, you may answer... Yes, that's right, in Poitiers we repulsed the Arabs... in 732. Keep that in your minds: 732..."

Some days the inspectors come, inspectors of all sorts... fat, wheezy ones, who only say a few words, puffing and blowing... nasty, livid, thin ones, who hiss out bittersweet or caustic remarks... and I, too, transform myself, I change at will my appearance, my age, my voice, my manner...

This inspector is a little hard of hearing... "*What* did that pupil answer?"... I immediately change the wrong answer... "Is that what she said? And yet I rather thought..." "No, Monsieur l'Inspecteur, the whole class heard her... Didn't you? (in honeyed tones), children?"... and the whole class, in chorus, bleat... "Oooui Maadaame..."

It's such a pity when I have to tell my pupils that school is over for today, and I have to gather up the paper birds and put them away side by side in their box.

I am in bed in my room in a villa in Meudon where we are spending the summer... The whole of my right arm, from shoulder to wrist, is swollen, hard, burning, covered in pustules, I have a very high temperature... this is the result of an injection the doctor here has given Lili and me to stop us from catching diphtheria. Lili is all right, but I... I hear someone say that he must have injected me with a needle that wasn't clean enough... I'm getting worse and worse, great big earwigs, insects I am very frightened of, are running all over me, are going to enter my ears, I scream... Papa speaks to me gently, his hand is on my forehead... every time I regain consciousness I stretch out my arm and feel him there, very close... He is the only one... Never

Vera...

—That seems barely possible... Really never?

—No, never, not during that illness, in any case...

—She must have quarrelled with your father...

—Probably. She often revenged herself like that by taking absolutely no notice of me. And when Vera had come
to a decision... you could have died...

—That seems the appropriate expression...

—It's nearly dark... All of a sudden, my father picks me
up, wraps me in a blanket and carries me, with the help of a
man... he was the driver of a taxi he had sent to Paris for...
The whole way, in his voice from the old days, he reassures
me, he strokes my head... "It'll be all right, you'll see, we're
going to see a great children's doctor, a professor, he will be
able to cure you..." The taxi stops in a wide Paris street,
they take me up, they carry me through some big salons
into an all-white room... a doctor examines me... he takes
some forceps and one by one cuts the pimples on my arm...

—You can still see the scars.

—He bandages me, he gives me an injection, he is very calm and gentle. My father and the taxi driver take me down. In the taxi, my father looks happy, he holds me tightly in his arms... "You're going to get well, Professor Lesage..."

—A name he often repeated... "Professor Lesage... what a doctor... I shall never forget him... Without him..."

—"Professor Lesage promised... What a good thing we went to him... you're going to sleep now, you'll soon be in your bed and it will all be over, you'll soon be well, Tashot-shek, my little girl, my darling."

For some time now, when I come out of school at four o'clock I no longer dawdle in the street, chatting, playing hopscotch, I want to hurry back, I know that she has heard the school bell and is expecting me... I don't go straight to my room down the corridor, I go first to her room, which opens on to the vestibule, I run up to her, I kiss her, I hug her, I call her babushka in Russian, and in French I call her grand-mère, she wanted me to, even though she is Vera's mother.

But no real grandmother could ever exist who would suit me better, be more to my liking. And yet, judging by appearances, she isn't very much like the delightful grandmothers described in books...

—Not a great deal in common with the one you later described in one of your own books...

—Nothing but the soft skirt, the occasional brown spots on the back of her hands, and, on her ring finger, that little

200

hollow at the joint... But her hair is a dull yellow, her eyes are not like blue enamel, they are a rather faded yellowish green, she has a big, pale face, with rather heavy features... it's impossible to mould her into the dainty little blue and pink statuette of the fairy tale grandmother... impossible to immobilize her... there is something perpetually changing, sparkling about her, something lively that immediately stretches out to whatever you bring up...

I put down my schoolbag and go to wash my hands in the cloakroom that separates our rooms, and then we have tea, she makes the tea on a little stove, and she brings out of her wardrobe a pot of carrot jam she has made from her own recipe, and which she and I are the only ones to appreciate... I tell her everything that has happened at school, and she makes it interesting, amusing, by her way of listening to it... It is with her that I learn the most tedious lessons... with her, even geography has its charm, I don't need my paper birds any more. She is the only person I have shown them to, and on one occasion I gave them a lesson in front of her, I made her laugh...

We both laugh a lot, especially when she reads comedies to me... *Le Malade imaginaire...* or *The Government Inspector...* she reads very well, sometimes she laughs so much that she has to stop, and I am literally doubled up with laughter, lying on the rug at her feet.

No one would believe that this is the first time in her life that she has been to France... Listening to her speaking, you would be sure that she has always lived here, there isn't the slightest trace of accent in her pronunciation, in her intonation, she never has to search for her words...

She just sometimes... rarely, though... uses certain

201

words that have an old-fashioned air... like *serrer* instead of *ranger* (to put away)... "*serre cela dans le tiroir de la commode*"...

It sometimes happens at meals that she forgets she is in France, and if she is speaking Russian and wants to say something that the maid serving at table isn't supposed to understand, she says it in French, and it is sometimes an uncomplimentary remark... then Vera reminds her in Russian that she is in France, and she blushes, and expresses her regret, in Russian this time... Good gracious! so I am, what am I thinking of? How awful...

My father calls her Alexandra Karlovna... Karl isn't a Russian first name, her father was called Charles Feue de la Martinière, he was a French officer sent on a mission to Russia by Napoleon (for a long time I believed it was Napoleon I, and I was terribly disappointed when I learned that it was Napoleon III). There he married a Russian girl, and soon afterwards they both died of cholera, leaving a daughter, Alexandra...

Our meals are transformed by her presence... between my father and her there is, I feel, respect, affection... my father talks to her a lot, and she too recounts, discusses, they ask each other questions, and they ask me about my studies, completely oblivious, and as if unaware, of Vera's presence, and I—as if nothing was happening—I reply. My father expresses the highest praise for the way the primary schools, judging by mine, treat and teach children... they are a model of education, these French schools... A country for which he feels a passion that he would like to get her to share.

After dinner I often go back into her room, she teaches

me to crochet one of the big round shawls with the large stitches which she makes for herself and which she always wears, folded in two, over her shoulders... I like to try to remember with her the German I learned to speak in the past, and she gets me to read it in the gothic script... She gives me piano lessons, which I enjoy far less, but she would be pleased if I could play, so I agree without complaint, sitting beside her, to start over and over again, never-endingly, the most boring things in the world, exercises and scales...

One day I asked her how she had learned all she knows, and she told me that after her parents' death, she had become a ward of the Tsarina and had been educated at the Smolny Institute... I had had a book in St. Petersburg whose story was set in the Smolny Institute... My mother thought it an insipid, inferior book... What do you see in it? But it fascinated me... I believe it even inspired one of the episodes in that unfortunate novel of mine in which I made a young consumptive die with the first breath of spring...

Sitting on the floor, leaning against Grandmother's knees, listening to her talking about her childhood, I could see again the vast, snow-covered squares with their blue glints, the colonnaded façades of the palaces painted in delicate colours, the tall double-windows, the layer of padding sprinkled with silver sequins between the windowpanes with their patterns traced by the frost, the sparkling stalactites, the sleighs... and in one of those palaces, the long wide galleries with their shiny parquet floors, the little white bedrooms... the pretty uniform, the strict rules... every other day, during the week, you speak nothing but French to each other... another day German... it is forbidden, even in a whisper at table or in a corridor, to utter a single word in Russian. Frenchwomen, German women, Englishwomen keep permanent watch and let nothing pass... And the feast days... the visit of the Tsarina... an apparition of pure beauty and goodness... the introductions, the curtseys... the ball in white dresses, with flowers in your hair... you couldn't be farther away from the little streets in Paris, from these houses with their flat grey façades, from our black overalls, from my school, from its classrooms, from its courtyard, from its cement playground with the good old face of President Fallières on the wall...

What more do you want me to tell you? It wasn't always much fun, it was often very cold, the rules were severe, I had no parents... "And after, when you had left?"... "Oh, after... I was married very young... to an officer..." I knew that her husband, Fyodor Cheremetyevsky, had taken to drink... someone, I don't remember who, certainly not she, had told me that he had died of a dreadful illness that makes you see horrible insects running around everywhere... delirium tremens... "After his death, when I was left on my own... he was a terrible spendthrift, he had ruined himself... I had to bring up our four children... I had to teach, to give lessons..." "Is that why you are so good at...?" "It couldn't be helped, I had no choice, they were still small... Fyodor, now..." Grandmother always speaks with pride about her oldest son... "Fyodor is a university professor... Genia is very well-educated... Lydia"... she doesn't much like talking about her... Vera sometimes says that this sister is a little odd.. and Vera herself... Grandmother calls her "la petite," she's her youngest... you can feel that she loves her...

—There doesn't seem to have been the slightest disagreement between them during the whole of this stay, never a cross word... When you come to think of it, it is amazing that Vera should have taken so well your very affectionate relationship with her mother... and also the fact that her mother didn't go near Lili often, or rather kept a distance from her... But Vera knew quite well that her mother was not much interested in very small children, and she must have realized that Lili's nervous temperament, her perpetual whims and her screaming, even kept her father away from her... It was only later that he became closer to Lili...

—You could feel that Vera loved her mother and had a great deal of respect for her, and that her mother was very fond of her but that she worried her a little, she must have been difficult to bring up... Grandmother said to me one day... this was perhaps the only time she spoke to me about her... "She is the image of her father... None of my other children is so like him... When there was something she wanted or didn't want to do, there was no way... she gets that from him... and also, her love of dancing, a real gift... and her intrepidity... *I* am more..." I take her in my arms, I hug her... "Oh, you, you, you are... Nobody could be better than you."

And then, just as suddenly as she had come, she went. Her son was begging her to return, he had three daughters she used to give a lot of time to, she had promised to come back after a few months, and it was now almost a year... she must return... she has told me so several times, but I couldn't take it in, it was impossible, I didn't want...

When, before she left, she took me in her arms, we were alone, I felt as if a cloud had descended on me... She held me a little way away from her so as to look deep into my eyes, she stroked my cheek, and she said: "Go on working well, that's the most essential thing." And then she added something that astonished me: "Take good care of your papa."

I have no recollection of the state her departure left me in... I could only imagine it, that would be easy. I remember with perfect clarity, on the other hand, how, some time afterwards, quite a long time afterwards, my father asked Vera in a rather worried tone... they were in the next room and didn't think I could hear them... "What is the matter with Natasha?" and she replied: "It's because Mama has gone."

Adèle sometimes used to take me to church in Montrouge, where I made the same gestures as she did... gestures which didn't seem to me to be very different from those required by pure politeness... the hand rapidly dipped into the font, the automatic sign of the cross, the perfunctory genuflexion as you passed the altar... she would have been very shocked if I hadn't, just as she would have been if I hadn't said "Au revoir Madame" when I went out of a shop... or if I hadn't stood aside in a doorway... It was impossible for me to imagine... in spite of all the acts of piety rigorously and very frequently performed by Adèle, she often went to the six o'clock morning service, never missed Mass on Sundays... I couldn't credit her with the slightest particle of a spiritual life, with any sort of feeling about the possible existence of anything that wasn't on earth, of the earth, on the level of the earth she lived on.

—But you yourself, when you prayed...

—It was more like superstition... I recited "Our Father

which art in Heaven," or "Holy Mary, Mother of God"...
in the same way as I touched wood, to ward off bad luck or
in the vague hope that, by doing so, I would get what I
wanted...

With Grandmother, in the Russian church in the rue
Daru, I used to prostrate myself by her side with my forehead on the ground, I made the sign of the cross, this time
not like with Adèle, from left to right with my hand open,
but from right to left with my thumb pressed against two
fingers.

I don't know whether Grandmother was really a believer,
I think she went to church on feast days to take part in the
rites she loved, to rediscover her Russia, to plunge back into
it, and I plunged back into it with her... I rediscovered the
warmth, the light of innumerable candles, the icons in their
shrines, like silver or gold lace lit by the flames of little coloured rush lights, the Gregorian chants... a pervasive fervour everywhere and a kind of very gentle, calm exaltation
in me which I had already felt... was it in St. Petersburg, or
even before that, in Ivanovo...

—It's strange that, at that age, it didn't occur to you that
these religions were not that of your ancestors... that no
one had ever spoken to you about it...

—My mother didn't want to know that... I don't believe
she ever thought about it. As for my father, he considered
all religious observances to be a kind of relic... old, out-
moded beliefs... he was a "free thinker," and for him, as for
all his friends, the very fact of mentioning that someone is
or is not a Jew, or that he is a Slav, was a sign of the darkest

reaction, a veritable obscenity...

I never heard it said of a friend who came to the house that he was anything other than Russian or French. And at school, even the very notion of Russian didn't seem to exist, all the pupils, no matter where they came from, were considered to be good little French children. I don't remember anyone ever asking me any questions... obviously, ideas of any difference of race or religion never entered anyone's head.

My father allowed me to go to all the churches anyone took me to... perhaps he said to himself that those lovely ceremonies could only leave the child with lovely memories, and he no more tried to steer me away from God, from Christ, from the saints, from the blessèd Virgin, than he had stopped me praying to Father Christmas.

But later, every time this question came up, I always saw my father immediately declare, shout from the housetops, that he was Jewish. He thought that it was vile, that it was stupid, to be ashamed of it, and he used to say: How many horrors and ignominious acts, how many lies and servile acts, has it taken to achieve this result: that people are secretly ashamed of their ancestors and feel of greater value in their own eyes if they can manage to claim others, no matter which, so long as they are not those. "Don't you agree?" he sometimes said to me, much later, "that all the same, when you come to think of it..." Yes, I did agree.

Madame Bernard never asked me any questions about my family life, she said to me as she did to the others: "Ask your Mama to come and see me..." she may have noticed that it was always Papa who came... in any case, I don't know why, one day she asked me whether I would like to come and have tea with her children the next day... and then stay on a little and do my homework at her house.

—Perhaps it was because of the incident... you remember... the lice...

—Ah yes, the lice... the classroom is still fairly empty, I am the only one in my row, and sitting behind me are the two worst pupils in the class, inseparable gossips, always whispering to each other, exchanging winks, giggling... I avoided them, but they played an important part in my class of paper birds... they were a great help to me when I was beginning to get bored, they gave me a chance to amuse myself by making them say preposterous things, give funny, insolent answers...

Now they are there in flesh and blood, sitting behind me, not in the least funny, a little repugnant, vulgar, whispering, giggling, malevolent... they stifle little screams, little laughs, and when I turn round they put on a wooden-faced act... The moment the lesson is over they rush down the steps, run up to Madame Bernard, and whisper something to her excitedly... and then I see Madame Bernard looking for me, she beckons to me, and she takes me into a little office next to the classroom. There she says: "Let me look at your head"... she bends over until she is very close to my hair and then, in embarrassed, scandalized, grave, compassionate tones, she utters these unexpected words: "You have lice... They will have to get rid of them for you as quickly as possible... For that, you will have to stay at home for a few days... A pupil will come and bring you everything you need to keep you abreast of things, and you can give her your homework, in that way, you won't miss anything... and ask your Mama to come and see me." And she gives me a preoccupied, penetrating and affectionate look which once again reveals to me the sensitivity, the great, discreet goodness I always feel in her...

I go home as quickly as I can and announce to Adèle and Vera the amazing news: "I have lice! Yes, in my hair..." Adèle rushes up, looks, undoes my plaits, confirms... "But how is it that you didn't feel anything? Doesn't it itch, then?" "Not at all..." "Jesus Mary Joseph, Holy Virgin have mercy on us, there are even nits"... This is the first time I have heard that word... Yes, there are nits, the eggs laid by lice... Vera grunts, flares up at Adèle, Adèle protests, accuses me... That's what comes of wanting to do everything herself... Mademoiselle does her own plaits, washes by herself, no one must touch her... While she is "answering Madame back," and Madame is furious, she is getting ready to go to the pharmacy, and she brings back an ointment and smears it over my head, dividing my hair up parting by parting, she completely saturates it, combs it up and squeezes it tightly in a towel.

Nothing emerged of the showdown that probably took place later between my father and Vera.

Personally, I found it hard to understand the excitement and giggles of the two pupils, Madame Bernard's grave, pre-occupied, embarrassed air, her tender, delicate compassion... and Adèle's emotion and protestations, Vera's furious accusations... I had the impression that I was always rather clean, and these lice in my head didn't seem to me to be very different from the microbes you catch, you can't help it, by contagion, as I had caught measles...

I don't know how many times I went to Madame Bernard's, whether I went there often... it has all melted into a few images... the glints of the yellowish green oilcloth that covers the big, square table in the dining room which is lit by a white opaline hanging lamp... Madame Bernard's face is a pink patch under the thick, silvery mass of her hair... her rounded, rather short body, her lively, precise gestures as she hands out, to her children and me, bars of chocolate, slices of buttered bread... the exercise books open in front of us, our hands... but I can't see us, I can only see arms, outstretched hands dipping pens into the heavy glass ink-well in the middle of the table... She is sitting in an armchair a little apart, knitting in silence... and from her posture, from the movements of her fingers, the slight click of her needles, from her gaze, which sometimes, when I raise my head, is resting on me with the same discreet attention... and tenderness?... no, not so much as that, and I prefer it not to be, it's more peaceful, more reassuring for the frontiers not to be crossed... they are some distance away, but not too far, they are at the right and proper distance... the limits of simple benevolence.

—This must have taken place, I think, before your grandmother's visit...

—Or was it after?

—No, before... it seems to me that your grandmother came when you were in the school leaving certificate class...

—In that class, the mistress was Mademoiselle de T.... I simply can't remember her name, I have a feeling that it was short, and ended in "y" or "é." Her adopted daughter, who was younger than me, was called, *that* I do remember, Clotilde.

Madame Bernard must have "passed me on" to Mademoiselle de T., because from the very first days I felt she showed an interest in me, a kind of sympathy... and later in the year, she sometimes asked me to walk home with her after school, it wasn't very far, somewhere on the same side of the rue d'Alésia, I wouldn't have any dangerous streets to cross on my way back.

She never asked me any personal questions either, we remained silent, or else we talked about what we were studying at school or about the books I read at home... like her, I got them from the library at the boys' primary school... We walk along the rue d'Alésia towards the parc Montsouris, she is holding Clotilde's hand... from time to time she stops, bends over me slightly with her elongated, thin bust, her flat-cheeked, very slender face, pushes back, as she often does, a strand of her dark brown hair which is falling over her forehead, over her lively eyes...

In class she articulated every word with extreme clarity, her explanations were slow, patient, repeated almost too often... With her, even more than with Madame Bernard, I had the impression of exploring... we can get there, we only have to make an effort... a world whose boundaries have been drawn with great precision, a solid world, visible all over... just made to my measure.

It was when I was still with Madame Bernard that I had a lump in my throat, tears came to my eyes, as they did to hers, when she was telling us about the 1870 war, the siege of Paris, the loss of Alsace-Lorraine. "The Marseillaise," which we sang in chorus, uplifted me, stirred me, I felt that its strains had captured the rage of an unbearable defeat, the desire for revenge, a warlike fervour...

With Mademoiselle de T., this admiration for the sacrifice of one's life in the service of one's country reached its climax...

The portrait of Bonaparte at the Arcole bridge, stuck into the frame of the mirror above my mantelpiece, charging, flag in hand, in itself summed up all my dreams of heroism and glory...

—It was a little later that you were filled with that great love for him...

—Was it love? I so identified myself with him... When, later, at the lycée, I pinned up on to the wall of my room a

215

huge map of the battle of Austerlitz, which I had myself drawn with crayons of all colours, I had put in every regiment, every hillock... it was I, incarnated in that rather plump, pot-bellied Napoleon, but I didn't see him, it was I, through him, who was looking through the spyglass, giving orders...

—When Mademoiselle de T. took the whole class to the Luxembourg museum and then gave as the subject for your French essay: "Describe the picture you liked best," naturally, the one you chose was *The Dream*, by Detaille...

—I still remember the sensation I had when I was describing in that essay the "battalions of heroes traversing a sky of glory above the soldiers asleep in their dark greatcoats..." a feeling of exaltation which spilled over into sentences I had taken from goodness knows where, they were already as inflated as one could wish, but it blew them up even more, so as to make them rise still higher... never high enough...

A student is bending over a table covered with exercise books and books, he is studying for an exam... when suddenly, behind his back, the dark velvet curtains half-open... two hands with thick, strong fingers emerge from them, advance... two hands wearing gloves made of a whitish skin... gloves made of human skin... slowly, they come nearer, they encircle the student's neck, they squeeze it... I'm dying, it's not the slightest use keeping the light on in my room, lying in my bed with my back pressed against the hard, bare wall, where there are no curtains... nothing can come from there... I can see the strangling hands, they're approaching my neck from behind... I can't stand it any longer, I jump out of my bed, I run along the corridor barefoot, I knock on the bedroom door, my father opens it, comes out, closing the door quietly, Vera is asleep... "Papa, oh please, let me stay with you, I'm frightened, I can't bear it any longer, I've tried everything, I can see the hands"... "What's the matter with you? What hands?" "The hands in the gloves made of human skin..." I sob... "please let me, I won't make any noise, I'll sleep on the bedside mat..." "You're crazy... That's what comes of... you go and see some idiotic film... you don't even ask permission..." "I did, I did ask you." "No, you didn't ask anything at all." "Yes, I did, I asked you whether I could go and see *Fantomas* with Misha, and you said, yes..." "It's not possible... what an idea... when someone is as easily frightened as you, I'm sure Misha isn't frightened..." "But *I* am going to die... only just thinking that it's going to come back, please stay with me..." "That's all I needed. I have to get up at six... and there's nothing wrong with you, you aren't ill, you lose control of yourself like a baby, a real sissy... at eleven years old, to have no more self-control than that, it's a disgrace. That's the last time you'll go to the cinema..."

I go back to my room, I get back into bed, I'm filled with rage at having exposed myself to such a humiliating rejection, such insulting contempt, it swells in me, I'm going to explode, I shall annihilate anything that dares approach me... hands... no matter what hands, even if they are wearing gloves of human skin... just let them come out... but while I'm getting back into bed and turning, not my back to the wall, what for? no, my back to the void behind me, on purpose, we shall see... it's no use shutting my eyes, bracing myself, waiting, my fury must keep them at a distance, they dare not come out behind *my* back, they are still there, nice and quiet, in the film, a long way from me... behind the back of that young man... hands... Misha was right... gloves made of human skin, those? But you can see that they are rubber gloves... thick rubber gloves... I laugh a little too loudly, I don't stop laughing, I cry with laughter as I fall asleep.

For some time now, Vera has seemed more re-
laxed, gayer than before, her lips are no longer permanently
pursed, her gaze is no longer so very hard and cutting, she
reminds me of how she used to be in the old days when she
danced with me in the rue Boissonade, or when she was
sitting with my father and me in the Luxembourg gardens,
by the lawns in the English garden...

—But since that time, which was already a long time ago,
it *had* happened, very infrequently, it's true, that she had
softened, become rejuvenated, as she had during those bi-
cycle rides in the forest of Fontainebleau, or when you
made her laugh by devouring enormous platefuls of pasta or
when she was excited and amused as she covered your
school books... well, there had been moments...

—And these moments now are even more delightful than the others, I feel something in Vera that I have never felt before... yes, attachment, affection... it must certainly have been there for a long time, but buried, shrivelled, hardened, and now it's coming out into the open, it's blossoming... and immediately my confidence, my affection... it takes so little to bring them out... well up in me, cover everything, overflow...

And so, when Vera offers to take me, I had been dreaming of it for such a long time, to see the famous fountains in Versailles, and suggests inviting two of my friends... "Which would you like best?" "Lucienne Panhard..." "And...?" "Claire Hansen, she's very gay, we play together during recreation, we can juggle with three balls, now... and just a bit with four..." "Oh, you must show me... we'll take a picnic..." "Oh, but... what am I going to do? Because Mama will be here... It will be two days after she arrives..." "Well, you can tell her... she'll understand perfectly, she'll be delighted to know that you are enjoying yourself..." "Do you really think so?" "I'm quite sure, what mother wouldn't be?... It's only for one day... Well, it's as you wish, I certainly wouldn't want..."

I only hesitate for an instant, and then I can't resist it, I am so strongly attracted, so drawn... "All right then, just too bad, I'll tell her, then we really will go?"

—Mama is here, she's going to spend August with me... she's expecting me, I'm going to see her... it's so long since I saw her, I was only eight...

—Exactly eight and a half, it was in February 1909.

—And on 18 July, I was eleven... and it seems to me that I am quite grown-up as I leave the house in the rue Marguerin and go alone, without support, to somewhere a long way away from here, where the people who live with me can't follow me... and even if they could, they wouldn't want to, it doesn't concern them, I'm the only one it concerns... But I am not very sure what I am going towards, it's imprecise, distant, almost foreign... and at the same time I know that no person on earth can ever be closer to me than the one I am going to meet... my mother, you only have one mother, what child is not supposed to prefer its mother to everything in the world? it's my mother I am going to meet...

Before I left, they explained to me...

—Today, you might have imagined that you were like a parachutist who is being dropped into space and being told one last time: "You're sure you'll remember, then, you won't make a mistake? you know what you have to do to get there?" and you say: "Yes, I know..." And behind you, the door closes.

—I follow all the instructions faithfully... I turn left into the rue d'Alésia until I come to the place de Montrouge, then left again into the avenue d'Orléans and, when I get to the porte d'Orléans, left once again, on the same pavement, two or three houses farther on, there will be a little hotel... and here it is, I can see it, it's the "Hôtel Idéal."

I go through the glass door and say to a fat lady sitting behind a counter on the right of the hall: "I would like to see Madame Boretzki"... and how bizarre the name sounds, it seems to me that this is the first time in my life that I have heard it...

—And yet in previous times, in the rue Flatters, that was how the name was said, in the French way...

—But that was such a very long time ago, an enormous space of time has elapsed between the ages of six and eleven... Now "Madame Boretzki," and also every word I say, has a strange, unreal sound... in contrast to the words the lady uses in reply, perfectly normal, commonplace words, in an indifferent, rather absent-minded tone: "Madame Boretzki is in," and she tells me the number of her room.

I knock on the door, I hear "Entrez!" and right away nothing is more familiar to me than that voice... deep, perhaps just a little raucous, and also the pronunciation, in which only the rolled "r" and a certain intonation betray the Russian accent.

I have a feeling that I wouldn't have recognized her if I had met her by chance... she has put on a little weight, but it is especially her new hair style, those two smooth, dark loops on either side of her forehead, like the ones Vera has... they don't suit her, they make her face, which was like no other, look a little commonplace, a little hard... But as soon as my lips touch her skin... I know no other skin like it, softer and silkier than everything soft and silky in the world, and her faint, delicious perfume... I want to stretch out my hand once again and caress her hair, but I don't dare, I'm afraid of ruffling it... her pretty, irregular, bronze eyes, one brow higher than the other, inspect me, I feel she is disappointed, I am not "pretty enough to eat," as people often used to tell me I was, she used to say it too, but no one says it any more... she shakes her head disapprovingly... "You look dreadful, you're so pale... It's that inhuman system... school until the end of July... And they cram knowledge into children, they turn them into little old men and women..." I remember that Mama doesn't attach much importance to schoolwork... she even rather despises it...

—She had often told you that she herself had been a bad pupil, always daydreaming... she seemed to be proud of it... She had told you how she had been expelled from the lycée for having had some tracts at home... but not out of revolutionary conviction, but because another pupil had asked her to, she hadn't realized the danger... and I believe she was convinced that she had better things to do... After she was expelled from the lycée, everything she knew she had learned from her reading...

—Even though I don't remember all these details while she is looking at me and telling me how unhealthy she considers the scholastic system here, I don't tell her anything about my school, or about my efforts, my successes...

She is half-lying on her bed, and I am sitting on a chair in front of her, it's extremely hot, she has pulled her dressing gown down over her shoulders, a bit too far, she is too naked, this shocks me a little, and then I remember that these are things which don't shock people in Russia as they do here... I see us again, both of us naked amongst other naked bodies of women and children, moving around in a dense, hot vapour, in the old days, in St. Petersburg, when I was with her at the *banya*.

We stay there facing each other, we look at each other, I don't know what to say, and I can see that Mama doesn't really know what to say either...

—And yet we had to talk to each other... What else could we do, what other way was there of getting to know one another again?

—Mama tells me: "Kolya sends you lots of love, he was so sorry not to be able to come, he's finishing a new book..." And then, she is silent, I can sense she's searching... "Do you remember the children you used to play with when we were in Razliv? Their dacha was next to ours..." "Yes. I still have the little flask with the little golden chain that you gave me for my seventh birthday..." "Well, would you believe it, I met their mother, the oldest boy, the one who was nine, is ill, he has tuberculosis of the bones, he has to stay in bed... But his little sister, she was the same age as you, you remember Valya? she is very well, it seems that she is still just as full of fun... Last summer we went on the Volga... I sent you some postcards... even a photograph of Kolya and me with a group of friends, on an excursion"... "Yes, I have them..." And Mama is still searching... hesitating...

—Like in a toy shop, with the sales assistant asking: For a

224

child of what age? Perhaps some building blocks? No? He's too big... Then a construction kit?

—Finally, she makes up her mind... "You know, over there, last summer, there was a fisherman who caught fish as big as that... We lit big wood fires with him, we cooked *oukhas*..." and then she stops, she senses that that isn't right for me... "But you aren't saying anything, tell me about yourself... You don't tell me anything in your letters... You have a little sister... how old is she exactly?" "She'll be two in August..." "She's called Lili?" "Yes." "But her real name?" "Hélène"... "Hélène?"... Mama seems shocked... I know that that is because it was the name of her daughter, of my "real sister," as I call her when I think about her, when I regret being so alone, not having her with me... In the far-off days when Papa, and Mama, too, sometimes, used to talk to me about her, they told me that you couldn't imagine a sweeter, more intelligent child... even too much so... people say of such beings that they were not created to live... "Hélène... but they don't call her Lola?" "No, they always call her Lili, both in French and in Russian..." "Ah, even so... I've heard that she is a difficult little girl, very nervous... and that that... Vera..." I flinch... I feel that once again Mama isn't very sure of whom she is talking to... now she no longer sees me as a child at all, she thinks she's talking to an adult... but I am not an adult, in any case, not the one she is seeing... "That... Vera," drawn out, dragged out by disdain, by contempt, is not for my personal use, it doesn't suit me, I don't want it...

—And yet you knew, as an adult would have known, that

there wasn't the slightest trace of jealousy, of envy in this contempt... you remembered Mama well enough to be sure that she could never experience anything of that order... she had never for a moment regretted having left, she must rather have felt sorry for the woman who had accepted the life that she herself had rejected, she was so profoundly satisfied with her own life... but, above all, Mama was always at such a great distance, too great for her ever to measure herself against anyone, compare herself with anyone at all...

—And that's what makes "that... Vera" even more distressing to me... That contempt comes from what Mama has been told by people she can trust, she could just as well have had some respect for Vera if she had been presented to her in a different light... The thing is, though, that Vera provokes, Vera deserves this contempt, and this hurts me, this frightens me, and I shrink back even farther, to a place where the words that are going to come won't be able to reach me... but Mama doesn't notice, she continues as if she were speaking to herself... "That... Vera isn't altogether normal... it seems she's an hysteric..."

This hits me very hard, it stuns me... what there is in that word... I can't quite see what it is, but it stirs up little ripples of terror in me, makes them run up and down me... I shake my head... "No? she isn't? So much the better, then... so much the better for you..."

And in a flash I feel, as I had never felt before, Mama's indifference towards me, it comes out in a spate from these words: "So much the better for you, then," it rolls me back, it hurls me back there, back to what, however bad it may be, does even so belong to me a little, is, even so, closer to me... it pushes me towards the woman who has replaced her, whom I am going back to, with whom I am going to live, with whom I do live...

How did I tell Mama that the next day... it was the day after her arrival... that I had to go to Versailles and that I would come and see her on my return? How did she react to that? How did the day with Vera, Claire and Lucienne go? I haven't the slightest recollection... where was my father? He had no liking for such Sunday outings, which, in any case, were extremely rare. He must have stayed at home, and read in his armchair...

—I wonder whether Vera had even told him about the plan... whether she told him anything afterwards... And you, did you mention it to him? I don't think so...

—In any case, on that particular Sunday... and this has never been effaced, I can see it with perfect clarity... when in the afternoon I ran to the "Hôtel Idéal" and asked downstairs if Madame Boretzki was in, I was told: "No, Madame Boretzki has gone out." "And when will she be back?" "She didn't say."

And the next morning, when I got to Mama's room, she told me that she was leaving, she was going back to Russia that very evening, she had already booked her seat on the train... But apart from that, all the words she said, the feelings she expressed, those I experienced... it has all long since sunk without trace... I can only imagine, having known it better since, her calm coldness, the impression of invincibility that she gave, as if she herself had been subject to an impulse which she found it impossible to resist... that was what my father must have felt when she left him... I understood this much later when he said to me, speaking not of her, but of "those people who"... there was no way of reaching her... I felt that she was already back there, very far away from me. It is unlikely that I even tried to hold her back.

I must have been paralyzed with amazement. Crushed under the weight of my offence, which had been heavy enough to provoke such a reaction. And perhaps I also felt a few spasms of revolt, of anger... I have no idea.

The one thing that emerges from oblivion and stands out is this: it was just before we parted and she is sitting by my side, on my left, on a bench in a garden or a square, there are trees round about... in the light of the setting sun, I am looking at her lovely pink and gold profile, and she is looking straight ahead of her, gazing into the distance... and then she turns to me and says: "It's strange, there are words which are equally beautiful in both languages... listen how beautiful it is in Russian, the word *gniev*, and how beautiful the French word for wrath, *courroux*, is... it's difficult to say which one has more force, more nobility"... she repeats, with a sort of happiness: *Gniev*... *Courroux*... she listens, she nods... "God, how beautiful"... and I reply: "Yes."

Immediately after Mama's departure we went, as we did

every summer, to live in a villa in Meudon... I probably looked overwhelmed, mournful and sad, and Vera and my father must have found this ridiculous, exasperating... and it must have been this, one fine day, not long after Mama's departure, that incited my father to come up to me, brandishing a letter... "Here, this is what your mother has written to me, look..." and I see, in Mama's big handwriting: "I congratulate you, you have managed to turn Natasha into a monster of egotism. I leave her to you..." my father snatches the letter out of my hands before I have finished reading it, he crumples it, crushes it in his fist and throws it as far away from him as possible, he makes a sort of cracking sound which shows that he is on the point of bursting with fury, with indignation... Haa...

Three years later, in July 1914, my mother is back. This time I live with her in Saint-Georges-de-Didonne, near Royan, in a pretty house where we have two bedrooms and a kitchen, overlooking a big orchard.

I had never seen anyone as radiant, as gay as she was, forever admiring the pine trees, the sea, the meadows, the trees, the flowers that surrounded us... she didn't like to pick the flowers, she preferred to look at them... she was always ready to enjoy everything, just as ready as I was to go off into fits of laughter...

"My house is not a mousetrap!"... this stock phrase, which Mama kept repeating, made us laugh until we cried... We had heard an actor say it with enormous grandiloquence in a melodrama played by a theatrical touring company... "My house"... and Mama stretched out an arm, threw back her head... "is not a mousetrap!" We found this hilarious...

And then, in August, the drum announced general mobilization. And after that, notices stuck up at the town hall informed us that we were at war. Mama was in a panic, she must go back to Russia immediately or she would be cut off, kept here... she could still take a boat leaving from Marseilles...

I went with her to Royan, to the train... I was heartbroken... and what broke my heart even more was her joy, which she didn't even try to conceal... the lovely trip to Constantinople... and then Russia and St. Petersburg and Kolya... how he must be longing for her, how worried he must be...

When I was back in the villa that my father and Vera had rented at the other end of Saint-Georges-de-Didonne, this time, too, my miserable air must have irritated them, my father was colder towards me than usual, and Vera even more hissing, more viperish than she quite often was in those days.

Shortly after Grandmother's departure, Vera decided that the moment had come when Lili absolutely must have an English governess. If they waited any longer, Lili wouldn't have the proper accent.

Not knowing English herself, she got one of her friends who knew about such things to make a thorough check on the way of speaking of all the young English girls who applied for the post, and to choose only the ones with the purest pronunciation.

Vera made it very clear to them that they were only engaged to look after "the little girl," "the big girl" didn't need them.

It quickly became apparent that nothing could more anger Vera, and turn her against them, than hearing one of them speak to me in English, make any sort of remark to me about my education, in short, than seeing them take the slightest bit of notice of me.

It seems to me now that this was perhaps an effort on her part to redress the balance of advantages, of opportunities, between Lili and me... I spoke very good Russian, a little

German, I didn't need English as well... What was more, a knowledge of English was for Vera a sign of distinction, of elegance, and it would put Lili a few points ahead of me. Also, perhaps, she considered that her mother had given far more to me than she had to her real granddaughter and that my father was rather too concerned with me...

In any case, if Vera had wanted to inspire me with a passion for English, she couldn't have gone about it in a better way... And then, it so happened that the language itself delighted me. And also, for the most part, I found them charming, those ingenuous young English girls, fresh blown from their country childhoods as the daughters of parsons, of schoolmasters... childhoods which could only have been what "real" childhoods are, lived in insouciance, in security, under the firm, benevolent guidance of united, fair and calm parents... They felt lost here, grappling with Vera's obscure passions and savage reactions.

They realized after a certain time that they occupied the "hottest seat," the most dangerous position in this house, they were in charge of Lili... Lili, who was protected against everyone by the powerful defence system drawn up around her by her mother... Those who even came near to committing the imprudence of letting Lili's snivelling and whining trigger this defence mechanism, which was in a permanent state of alert, had to beat a hasty retreat... If they dared to defend themselves, they came in for a volley of machine gun fire—these words, flung at them by Vera in her unanswerable tone: "Li-li-ne-ver-lies."

Few of them managed to hold out for long in this hot seat which, in Vera's presence, I approached as little as possible. But I didn't deprive myself when Vera wasn't there, which was quite often the case.

Especially in the evenings, when Vera and my father had

gone out, we came together, these lonely young English girls and I, in their room near mine, the one Grandmother had occupied, which had the advantage of being closer to the front door... from there it was easier to hear the sounds on the stairs, the street door closing, the steps coming up... they stop on the landing... the key fumbles in the lock, it's going to open... I must tear myself away from the joy of listening to this language, of trying to speak it myself, of discovering through those tender, nostalgic stories, as through the delightful nursery rhymes and the little children's books intended for Lili, a country in which everything charms me, awakens tenderness, nostalgia in me too... but there isn't a moment to lose, I take to my heels and close my door quietly...

—You remember Miss Philips, whom you met much later...

—It must have been about twenty years after she had left... I saw her in the Bois de Boulogne, in a nanny's navy blue uniform, pushing a baby's pram... I recognized her at once, and she seemed agreeably surprised to see that I had managed to survive... She said: "I still see your stepmother in my nightmares," and we parted, laughing.

They have put an old chest of drawers in my room, it was bought from a junk dealer and is made of dark wood, with a thick slab of black marble on top, a strong smell of must and mould emanates from its open drawers, they contain several enormous, hardbound volumes covered in black paper with yellowish marbling... the dealer has forgotten or perhaps not bothered to take them out... they are a novel by Ponson du Terrail, *Rocambole*.

All my father's sarcastic remarks... "It's rubbish, he isn't a writer, he wrote... personally I have never read a single line... but it seems that he wrote grotesque stuff... 'Her hands were as cold as a snake's'... he's a cheat, he didn't care about his characters, he mixed them up, he forgot them, in order to remember them he was obliged to represent them with dolls, which he shut away in his cupboards, he pulled them out haphazard, one he had killed off comes back a few chapters farther on well and truly alive... you surely aren't going to waste your time..." There's nothing doing, as soon as I have a spare moment I can't wait to get back to those big pages, buckled, as if they were still a bit wet, dotted with greenish patches, from which something intimate, secret, emanates... a mellowness rather like that which later enveloped me in a house in the provinces, decaying, ill-ventilated, everywhere there were little staircases, hidden doorways, dark recesses...

Here at last is the longed-for moment when I can spread the volume out on my bed, open it at the place where I was forced to abandon it... I throw myself on it, I plunge... impossible to allow myself to be stopped, held back by the words, by their meaning, their aspect, by the movement of their phrases, an invisible current carries me along with those to whom the whole of my being—imperfect as it is, but avid for perfection—clings, they are goodness, beauty, grace, nobility, purity and courage itself... with them I must confront disaster, brave horrifying dangers, fight on the edge of precipices, be stabbed in the back by daggers, be shut away from the world, ill-treated by frightful shrews, threatened with being lost forever... and each time, when we have reached the breaking point of my endurance, when there is no longer the flimsiest hope, the slightest possibility, the frailest chance... it happens to us... an insane courage, nobility, intelligence arrive just in time to save us...

This is a moment of intense happiness... always very brief... the agonies, the torments soon have me in thrall once again... obviously, the most valorous, the most beautiful, the purest have so far been saved... so far... but how can one not fear that this time... it has happened to beings who were only slightly less perfect... yes though, even so, they *were* less perfect, and they were less attractive, I was less attached to them, but I had hoped that for them too, they deserved it, at the last moment there would be... no though, they, and with them a part of myself, were thrown headlong from the top of the cliff, crushed, drowned, mortally wounded... for Evil is there, everywhere, always ready to strike... It is as strong as Good, at every moment it's on the point of conquering... and this time all is lost, all that is most noble, most beautiful, on earth... Evil has become firmly established, it has neglected no precautions, it has nothing more to fear, it is savouring its triumph in advance, it is taking its time... and it is at this moment that I have to reply to voices from another world... "We've been calling you, dinner's ready, didn't you hear?"... I have to go into the midst of these small, reasonable, prudent people, nothing ever happens to them, what *can* happen in the place they live in... everything there is so narrow, petty, parsimonious... whereas where we come from at every moment we can see the most beautiful palaces, mansions, furniture, bibelots, gardens, such as you never see here, streams of pieces of gold, rivers of diamonds... "What has happened to Natasha?" I hear a friend who has come to dinner ask my father in a low voice... my absent, haggard, perhaps disdainful air must have struck her... and my father whispers in her ear... "She's immersed in *Rocambole*!" The friend nods, as if to say: "Ah, I see..."

But what can they see...

In Vanves, at the corner of two long, dismal streets, in a dirty grey stone house, similar to the exterior of the other houses, my father is trying to reconstitute, on a much smaller scale, the "Dyestuff Manufactory" he had in Ivanovo.

Behind the house there is a tamped earth courtyard, surrounded by little sheds, where I can smell, as I did in the courtyard that stretched out in front of the vast wooden buildings in Ivanovo, a nauseating stench of acid, and, as I did there, I have to step over rivulets of red, blue, yellow liquid... Passing the open door of a little office, I recognize on a table the big abacus with the yellow and black balls that you move up and down the rods. In the laboratory, my father, wearing white overalls, is bending over a table on which, in front of the test tubes standing in their wooden supports, the retorts, the lamps, there is a line of glass slabs... on two of them, there is a little pile of bright yellow powder... I know, because my father often talks about it, that it is called "chrome yellow"... He observes one of the little piles for a long time... "Look carefully, don't you think that this one is less bright than the other? It's a little bit more greyish..." I try hard to see a difference... "No, I don't see... or perhaps I do, just a little..." "A little too much so, it's obvious, it's duller... It doesn't matter, I think I know why, we'll make it again... but that's enough for today, come on now, let's go..."

We go down the stairs, we're going to say goodbye to Monsieur and Madame Florimond. They work here and they live on the ground floor, facing the street.

I didn't often see them, but, curiously enough, their image is impressed on my memory far more clearly than the images even of the people I knew best... I think this is because, for me, "the Florimonds" seemed to be the exact reproductions of the images imprinted in me by my father with all his conviction, his passion... clear, simple images... like illuminated manuscripts, pious images... like illustrations of the qualities my father respects... On Monsieur Florimond's face, his crest of hair, his neck, his hands, which seem to be impregnated with red dye, I see his love of his work, he forgets to take precautions... what passes through his reddened eyes and flows into my eyes is his intelligence... many scientists might envy him that... is his candour, his pride... and Madame Florimond with her plump body, her chubby cheeks, her mouth, which her smile lifts higher on one side, her big, watchful eyes... is the image of devotion, of modesty, but also of steadfastness... And how they love each other... a trace of melancholy comes into my father's voice when he speaks of the touching care they take of each other... "marvellous people, I don't know what I would have done without them, I have no better friends than they, it is great good fortune"... They lean over towards me, they pat my head... "Isn't she like you"... My father is waiting for me in the doorway... He is silhouetted there, very slender and upright, he, too, is an image, that of determination and energy... his face is younger and happier than usual... He says: "Good. See you tomorrow, then"... a "Good" through which a little satisfaction escapes, a "Good" in which I perceive: "How good it is, what a good thing that it should be as it is, that I have today had my share of daily effort, that I shall have it again tomorrow... Without that daily effort, how is it possible to live?... Good. See you tomorrow, then... Come on, my daughter."

This is what he sometimes calls me since I have been in Paris, when he is being affectionate with me. Never Tashok any more, but, my daughter, my little girl, my child... and what I feel in these words, without ever spelling it out to myself, is something like the rather painful affirmation of a special bond that unites us... like the assurance of his constant support, and also a little like a challenge...

—But do you really think, even at that particular moment, in that remote haven, that sanctuary, under the protection of those holy images, that you saw in those words...

—I don't think that even then I could have heard my father call me "My daughter" as if I were hearing simple, ordinary, banal words, quite natural words that go without saying, the ones Monsieur and Madame Florimond heard.

We are coming back, Vera and I, from the avenue d'Orléans where we have been shopping, we are walking calmly down the rue d'Alésia, a few steps farther on we shall cross it and go into the rue Marguerin... when all of a sudden I put my hand on Vera's hand, which is holding her long skirt up a little, and I ask her point-blank: "Tell me, do you hate me?"

I knew very well that Vera wouldn't reply: "Yes, I hate you"... I must have hoped that this violent word, unexpectedly flung at her, would catch her, bring her closer to me, she would be forced to turn round, to plunge a rueful look deep into my eyes and say: "What on earth are you talking about? Quite the contrary, come on, how can you not feel that?"

—No, there you're going too far, you couldn't have expected such effusions...

—Then I wanted her at least to give me an irritated look,

241

to shrug her shoulders and say: "What a stupid question! Really, when you hear such things it makes your ears wither"... A Russian expression she often used...

Well, what is certain is that I was expecting something, that I was begging for a reassuring little pat.

—And you may well have been trying to take advantage of that period of calm, of harmony, to frighten her: "You see, look, now, when you're behaving so well, just observe what sometimes happens in you, that seething, that hissing, those sudden suppressed rages that come over you goodness knows where from... perhaps from the mere fact of my presence... look, that *is* the name people give it: "hate," that *is* what it's called. It's obvious, you "hate" me... Don't you? It isn't obvious? It isn't that? You don't hate me? What is it, then? Let's try and examine it together... in all sincerity... let's put our hearts together... I'm quite prepared to see what you see in mine, and you too... with the same fervour, in the same spirit, we shall...

—Yes, there must have been something like that in it, however incredible it may seem...

Vera stops abruptly, she remains silent... and then she says in her curt, peremptory tone: "How can anyone hate a child?"

Words she went to fetch, and which she brought back from a place where I can't follow her... compact, opaque words in which I can only perceive the "anyone" that I recognize... "Anyone"... normal people, moral people, people who are as they should be, people like her...

242

And "hate"... what a word!... one of those words that are too vehement, in bad taste... that a well-brought up child should not use, and above all, what presumption... should not dare to apply to herself...

"Do you hate me?"

But who does this child take herself for? "Hate!" how can a child arouse such a feeling?

There are still a lot of things in store for me before anyone can "hate" me... I still have quite some time to wait before I can obtain that promotion...

But later, when I no longer belong to this category of pathetic pygmies who make irrational, uncoordinated gestures, whose minds are still unformed... later, if what is already in me still subsists... something I don't see, but which *she* sees... if it remains in me, the thing that no one can hate now, no one can hate a child... but when I am no longer a child... but if I were not a child... ah, well *then*...

I go hurtling down, rolling over in the short, luxuriant grass strewn with little mountain flowers, to the river Isère, which is sparkling down below the meadows, between the tall trees... I kneel by its bank, dip my hands into its transparent water, moisten my face with it, lie down on my back and listen to it flowing, I breathe in the odour of wet wood given off by the enormous trunks of the stripped pines carried along by its current and washed up near me in the tall grass... I press my back, my arms outstretched, as hard as I can against the moss-covered earth so that all its saps can penetrate me, so that they will spread throughout my body, I look at the sky as I have never before looked at it... I melt into it, I have no limits, no end.

The fog, which comes right up to the hotel, envelops the meadows, fills the valley, is beneficial, it softens, makes less painful the end of the holidays... Its freshness, its greyness, stimulate me, they strengthen my impatience to confront, finally, what is awaiting me at the start of the school year, that "new life" at the lycée Fénelon, I have been told that you have to work very hard there, that the teachers there are very demanding, you'll see, it may well be difficult to begin with, you'll find it very different from your primary school...

Finally, very early one morning, Vera takes me to the corner of the avenue d'Orléans and the rue d'Alésia, where the Montrouge-Gare de l'Est tram stops... She helps me up the step, leans over towards the door and says to the conductor: "If you please, this is the first time that *la petite* has taken the tram on her own, will you be kind enough to remind her to get off at the corner of the boulevard Saint-Germain..." she tells me once again to take care, I reassure her with a gesture and go and sit on the wooden bench by the window, putting my heavy new schoolbag, crammed full of new exercise books and text books, down on the floor between my legs... I stop myself jumping up all the time, I turn from one side to the other to look at the streets through the dusty windowpanes... it's infuriating that the tram waits so long at each stop, that it doesn't go faster...

—Don't worry, I've finished, I won't take you any farther...

—Why now, all of a sudden, when you haven't been

afraid to come this far?

—I don't really know... I don't feel like it any more... I'd like to go somewhere else...

It may be because I feel that this, for me, is where my childhood ends... When I look at what is facing me from now on, what I see is something like an enormous, very congested, very well-lit space...

I couldn't go on making the effort to conjure up a few moments, a few movements, that I feel are still intact, still strong enough to emerge from the protective cover they are preserved under, from those soft, whitish, cloudy layers which dissipate, which disappear with childhood.